TRAVELS with TOM CREAN

Antarctic Explorer

Aidan Dooley

with Aileen O'Brien

The Collins Press

First published in 2016 by
The Collins Press
West Link Park
Doughcloyne
Wilton
Cork
T12 N5EF
Ireland

Paperback ISBN: 978-1-84889-283-5
PDF eBook ISBN: 978-1-84889-593-5
EPUB eBook ISBN: 978-1-84889-594-2
Kindle ISBN: 978-1-84889-595-9

Typesetting by Carrigboy Typesetting Services
Typeset in Palatino and Dirty Headline
Printed in Malta by Gutenberg Press Limited

CONTENTS

PROLOGUE

We Irish believe that our land is greener than anywhere else. It's obviously not, but still, we believe it. And it looked very green to me that autumn day when I arrived in Kerry at Farranfore Airport. There were no clouds as we flew in over Munster. I remember picking out the Knockmealdown Mountains, the MacGillycuddy's Reeks, all the peaks I learned about at school. Home. I was going home; I was bringing Tom home. I have flown into Ireland hundreds of times but this felt different. I thought about all the people who were converging on Tralee, on their way to see me, actor Aidan Dooley, step into the mighty shoes of polar explorer Tom Crean. I was terrified. 'Who do you think you are?' I asked myself.

I didn't even begin to suspect that this was the beginning of a journey that would last over a decade and take me all over the world. Since that weekend in Kerry in 2001, I have performed my show, *Tom Crean – Antarctic Explorer*, in all sorts of places and spaces: in vast theatres and remote rural halls, in Dublin and Dubai, Australia and Antibes, off Broadway and on the Antarctic ice itself. And, of course, time and again Tom and I have returned to Ireland, where he has been given his due hero's welcome by audiences up and down the country. It has been an extraordinary journey.

This is the story of me and Tom Crean, of how I came to write and perform the play that has changed my life, won an award or two, and of the adventures, challenges and people I have met along the way.

Like my show, this is, above all, a tribute to a remarkable polar explorer, the Kerryman who stood shoulder to shoulder with Scott and Shackleton on three legendary trips to the South Pole and performed feats of such courage and fortitude that they simply defy belief. This is for Tom Crean, a true Irish hero.

1
TOM WHO?

There are times, not yourselves now, mostly beyond, when I stand out here like this and many, no, most, don't know who I am, yet I've been there three times. I'll ask, 'Have you heard of Captain Robert Falcon Scott?' I tell you, a penny to a pound, most of 'em will nod the head, 'Oh yes, we heard of him.' He only went twice! I'll then ask, 'Have you heard of Sir Ernest Shackleton?' About three quarters will nod their head at him. 'Well, surely, surely,' I say, 'you must have heard of Tom Crean?' Arrgh … They look at me like I've got four heads. But 'tis my own fault, I never kept a diary: no diary – forgotten. Between you and me, I had more things to be doing at minus 30 degrees centigrade than writing a flaming diary.

From *Tom Crean – Antarctic Explorer* (Aidan Dooley)

Amid the stark, imposing landscape of the South Pole and Antarctic, there is both a mountain and a four-mile glacier bearing the name Crean. It was here that the son of a Kerry farmer distinguished himself as one of the great explorers of the Heroic Age, his name justly stamped forever on the unforgiving terrain that could not break him. But a hundred years later, this name was unfamiliar to most people. It certainly meant nothing to me when I first heard of Tom Crean.

It was early in the year 2000. I was working in London's Science Museum as an actor doing 'live interpretations'. This involved playing a character, historical or imagined, who would entertain and hopefully educate the visitors who strolled around the exhibitions. On this particular day I was just about to get into Edwardian costume to greet people as Victorian plumber Thomas Crapper and talk about my sanitary ware, as you do when you're a museum actor. My boss, Geraint, came to me and said that the Maritime Museum was staging a big exhibition the following year on polar explorers Scott and Shackleton and they'd found this fella, this Irish fella, who had gone to the Antarctic with both of them. His name was Tom Crean and he was one of the few men who had served under both Scott and Shackleton on their legendary polar expeditions:

Scott's *Discovery* (1901–1904) and *Terra Nova* (1910–1913) expeditions and Shackleton's *Endurance* (1914–1916) trip. As Geraint explained, the idea was to bring to life this unknown character, Crean, who would greet visitors and tell them about these polar expeditions while comparing the very different leadership styles of the two explorers: the buttoned-up, regimented approach of the Royal Navy's Scott and the more easy-going, approachable style of merchant navy man Shackleton.

It sounded like an interesting idea, but there was one problem. While his famous bosses had series of books dedicated to them, there wasn't a word written about Tom Crean. Geraint gave me by way of background a couple of pieces of A4 paper with little more than the diaries of the men with whom he reached the South Pole. The Irish

actor, along with fellow actor John ..., performed a twenty minutes of ... ... in costume as Tom ... ... at the Maritime ... ... of what we'd ... ... was and the ... ... version of ... ... were all in a boat and it was very tough but we did it, and thanks very much. The audience weren't to know the nine minutes I gave them should have been twenty, and they went away happy.

Over the next six or seven months, I performed the Tom Crean character regularly at the Maritime Museum. I built up my knowledge of his three polar expeditions and would vary which one I put into the show, but mainly it was the two Scott trips, as they could be told more succinctly and fitted more easily into my short time slot. Although the origina brief was to compare the leadership styles of Sc and Shackleton, I didn't make this the cen focus of the piece. Instead, I concentrated more putting the Antarctic in context for those who k nothing about it – for example, how the men in temperatures of minus 40 °C. It was going well with visitors and I was enjoying playir But it wasn't until a few months later, wher copy of Michael Smith's excellent book *A Hero*, that I really got the true measure o This first-ever biography of Tom Crean, as luck would have it, just the year bef really brought home to me just what he l in the Antarctic. I read about Crean who, time and again, defied death a magnificent feats to save his comrad

Aidan's first performance as Tom Crean at the National Maritime Musem, Greenwich, London in 2000.

and mental strength was matched by a clear head under pressure, an unfailingly cheerful disposition and enormous courage. I now understood why he was highly regarded by both Scott and Shackleton.

During his second Antarctic trip with Scott, Crean dodged killer whales and risked his own life to jump precariously over disintegrating ice floes and get help for two colleagues stranded on the ice. And during this same ill-fated *Terra Nova* expedition, it was Tom Crean who, starving and exhausted after months on the punishing ice, summoned the strength for an astonishing 35-mile solo journey to save the lives of his desperate comrades, Teddy Evans, who was dying of scurvy, and the exhausted Bill Lashly. This incredible trek earned Crean the rare honour of an Albert Medal, one of only 568 ever awarded during its 105-year history. And Crean was one of the few who found the desolate, frozen tent that bore witness to the tragic end of Robert Falcon Scott's race to the South Pole. During the *Endurance* expedition, when the boat was lost and the men were stranded, Crean was one of the trusted men chosen by Shackleton to accompany him on a life-or-death rescue mission that included a hair-raising trek across the mountains and glaciers of South Georgia, where no human had ever ventured before.

Yet, a century later, hardly anyone had heard of Tom Crean. Indeed, he had only merited one brief reference in the Maritime Museum's major exhibition of polar explorers. And I thought to myself, here was this English institution paying no mind to him at all. But, to be fair, the Irish didn't know about him either. Most would have been like me: 'Oh really? There was an Irishman with Scott? I didn't know that.' I was appalled by the injustice of it and I was inspired to redo my show entirely. As an Irishman, I wanted people to know about Tom Crean; I wanted to honour his achievements. As an actor and writer, I also felt that his story had the dramatic potential to be very powerful.

I began working on a less educational and more emotional version, investing in Tom's character so that the audience could, too. At the same time, coincidentally, the museum started to book the show into a self-contained room so I no longer had to perform it in the vast, echoing atrium where I had to fight to hold people's attention. The Submarine Room, where the children usually came to sit and have their lunch, even had a couple of lights that I could turn on and off. Most importantly, it had a door that could be shut to create a little world, our own polar fantasy, if you like. Before long, I had lengthened the performance to nearly an hour and it felt like a real, layered piece of drama. Museum characters are usually based on education through laughter and suddenly I was able to make people feel other things, too. I was getting great responses and feedback from the audiences and the museum was very pleased with it.

Apart from the notable absence of Tom Crean, the Maritime Museum's polar exhibition, called South, was fantastic, with many original artefacts borrowed from all over the world. But sooner or later the keepers of the pieces would need them back, so we knew the exhibition – and therefore my museum show – could not go on forever. In the meantime, the marketing manager and Jane Dewey of the education team came up with the idea of taking Tom back to his home in order to drum up some press attention for the remaining months of the exhibition. They contacted the Kerry County Museum in Tralee because of its proximity to Annascaul, the village on the Dingle Peninsula where Tom was born and where he returned after retiring from the Royal Navy. Tralee agreed to take the show and put it on in the theatre there. It was also arranged that I would then take it to Annascaul and perform it in the South Pole Inn, the pub Tom bought for his retirement and where he lived with his wife, Ellen, and daughters from 1920 until his death in July 1938.

So that's how I found myself on a plane heading for Kerry on a bright autumn day. I had never performed anything I'd written outside of a museum before and as I looked out over Munster, I had no idea if *Tom Crean – Antarctic Explorer* would stand up in a different setting – and on Tom's home turf, too. There were some considerable people coming to see it. As well as the team from the Maritime Museum and some journalists, the audience would also include Tom Crean's daughters, Mary and Eileen. I wasn't trying to impersonate Tom and I have a very different energy from him. I could imagine his daughters saying, 'My father wasn't like that, he didn't do any of that. Will you stop leaping around, what are you doing with your hands and, Jesus Christ, will you just stop it?' That's what nerves will do to you.

And I thought of my parents, on their way from Galway to see me. This was first time they had seen me perform professionally in Ireland since I had given up my very steady, very secure job at Allied Irish Bank fourteen years earlier to train to be an actor. And my Irish debut was to be in a theatre foyer and a room above a pub. It wasn't the most impressive setting. If I'm honest, I was also trying to forget that I was being paid a pittance – a mere £60 a day – for my performances, my script and all this pressure. But then again, I thought, it's three days in Tralee and I've never been to Tralee.

The plane was an hour and a half late so I felt even more stressed when I arrived at our first venue. 'So why are you doing it out here?' asked the mystified theatre manager. We were in the foyer of the Siamsa Tíre, the national folk theatre of Ireland. The foyer was the least theatrical space you could imagine, the sort of area where they display art or posters on felt boards. The Maritime Museum had suggested I do the show there because I was used to performing in non-theatre spaces. But even so, a foyer? 'Ah Jaysus, we'll put you on the stage,' said Martin, the manager. The stage, I discovered, was inside a 400-seater theatre, home of the Siamsa Tíre dancing company that has produced many Riverdance performers. It was certainly an improvement on the foyer as a theatrical setting and really added to the sense of occasion – giving me a thrilling shot of adrenaline as I looked out from the stage to the auditorium.

I had brought over a travelling version of the show in suitcases – essentially a tarpaulin and the costume I still wear over a decade later, the same boots, gloves, long johns, jumper and trousers. My outfit is topped by a Burberry: not the smart fashion rainwear it is today, but rather a windproof gaberdine outer garment made especially by Burberry for Antarctic explorers. A BBC costumier friend of mine made a replica for me for the show. I had imagined that my costume was all I would have in the way of theatrical effects. But there was a wonderful stage manager at the Tralee theatre called Jimmy who said, 'Shall I throw a couple of lights at it?' So he did. 'Do you have any set?' he asked. I did not. He came up with a big rock they'd used as set in an Irish dance piece. It had a handy little step in it where I could perch my bottom during the show. So there I was, ready to go. The show was supposed to start at 5 p.m., but because of our delayed flight, the PR team from the Maritime Museum and the journalists with them were still getting ready over in the hotel. There were around 40 people outside the auditorium waiting to come in and the clock was ticking. When, eventually, everyone had arrived and sat down, the museum manager introduced the piece. But I was dismayed that he made it all about me rather than Tom Crean, how I was from the historic area of The Claddagh in Galway City and had given up my job in the bank to become an actor. His introduction set entirely the wrong tone, so it was up to me to take the audience to the Antarctic. And out I went onto that stage.

As a performer, you know when you have an audience. You can feel their attention, their stillness. There's no coughing or fidgeting and, on cherished rare occasions, you can hear the proverbial pin drop. And so it was, on that night, in that theatre, in Tralee. I could certainly feel moments of silent intensity during the show. But, in all honesty, I didn't know if it was just the audience being respectful. And while I was very conscious of this extraordinary stillness, that it felt very special, I also assumed this was because I was at last doing the show in a dedicated theatrical space rather than a room in a noisy museum. So when I took my bow at the end, relieved to have got through it, I had no idea quite how much the audience had loved it, that they had, in fact, all been blown away by the show. My parents were delighted, as were Tom's daughters, Eileen and Mary, who were sitting in the front row. Mary, then in her eighties and still an elegant woman, said she thought it was wonderful, that she would never forget it and that I even looked like her father. I don't look anything like Tom Crean, but this was high praise that I was very happy to accept.

There was a question-and-answer session afterwards and I remember a woman with a turban and a posh Irish accent becoming really fired up about the fact Tom was a local man and how it was

Aidan with Tom Crean's daughters Mary (*left*) and Eileen Crean O'Brien (*right*) after the first time he played Tom Crean on a proper theatre stage at Siamsa Tíre in Tralee, County Kerry in 2001.

ridiculous that no one knew about him. There was no mention of him at all in the Tralee museum at that time, though if you go there today, you can now enjoy the Tom Crean area. Turban lady was all for setting up a Crean Society. It was all very positive and encouraging and it confirmed my feeling that Tom's story would make a potent piece of theatre. I was feeling delighted with myself when the local town councillor stood up and announced that I

Antarctic explorer Tom Crean bought a pub, the South Pole Inn, when he retired to his home village in County Kerry

Irish village hears tale of its forgotten polar hero

Greenwich exhibition tells of quiet man who came home to run a pub

Maev Kennedy Arts and
heritage correspondent

Captain Scott froze to death in 1912 on his second south pole expedition and is buried in his tent under a cairn of stones.

Ernest Shackleton died of a heart attack in 1922 on his aborted fourth south pole expedition and is buried in a whalers' graveyard on South Georgia.

Tom Crean, an Irish farmer's son who went three times to the Antarctic with both men, returned to his birthplace, the Kerry village of Annascaul, and opened the South Pole Inn. He is buried in a country graveyard in a tomb he built himself.

This week villagers and relatives of Crean joined a team from the National Maritime Museum in Greenwich, London, to visit the rain-sodden graveyard.

On Crean's grave is a wreath of porcelain flowers, sent 63 years ago by Lieutenant Teddy Evans. When Evans had been on the point of death from scurvy, Crean saved his life by walking 30 miles alone, with three biscuits in his pocket, to get help.

Village legend has it that the

wreath was delivered to Crean's funeral in a Rolls Royce.

Back in the South Pole Inn, actor Aidan Dooley told Crean's story to an audience that included his daughters, Mary and Eileen. The actor has been recreating Crean's adventures at the Greenwich museum, where a record-breaking exhibition on Antarctic exploration has been extended until January to cater for the crowds.

Unlike the stories of other explorers, that of Crean is little known in Ireland and almost unknown elsewhere, but that is to change. He is an important character in the Imax film opening in London this week, and in films by Kenneth Branagh and Russell Crowe about Shackleton, both due for release next year. Michael Smith, a former Guardian journalist, has written the first biography, and a documentary is being made. Annascaul, famous only for its horse fairs, is preparing for a tourist invasion.

The storytelling session at the inn was a unique event. Among the audience were children, grandchildren and great grandchildren of Crean's,

innumerable cousins, and villagers who remembered the man who went to the end of the earth three times. Mary and Eileen Crean, in their 80s, listened with tears in their eyes as Dooley launched into the tale of their father's 800 mile journey with Shackleton in a tiny open boat across some of the stormiest seas in the world — an epic still regarded as the greatest feat of open boat navigation — before they crossed the unmapped frozen mountains of South Georgia in a 36 hour non stop climb to get help.

While Crean was alive the inn had been the one place in Annascaul where these stories were never told. The pub was ruled over by his formidable wife, Nell. Everyone in Annascaul agrees that, although Crean spoke of his travels to village children and some

Tom Crean in his days as companion of Scott and Shackleton. Below, his gravestone in his home village of Annascaul Photographs: Frank Hurley (above) and Don MacMonagle

friends, for the remaining 20 years of his life he mostly sat quietly in the corner reading the paper, permitted the occasional half pint of Guinness by Nell.

Mary and Eileen live in nearby Tralee, side by side in houses called Terra Nova and Discovery, after the ships their father never told them his stories. "He put his medals and his sword away in a box on the wardrobe and that was that. He was a very humble man," Eileen said. Mary, fiercer of the two (villagers recognise Nell in her), is outraged that so little has been made of his story.

Tourists who make the trek up the potholedroad to the graveyard will not find a sign on the gate to say that one of the most remarkable figures in the Antarctic story is buried there. Perhaps that will change.

An October 2001 article by Maev Kennedy for *The Guardian* documenting Aidan's first trip to Ireland with the play, which was organised by the National Maritime Museum, Greenwich.

would be performing the show the next night at the South Pole Inn in Annascaul and would anyone be going to see it again. They all put up their hands – every one of them. And I thought, 'Oh God, I'm going to have to do the Shackleton story.'

2
A TALE OF ENDURANCE

Twenty-eight men stranded on a lump of ice, eight hundred mile from where we're supposed to be, a thousand miles from any other human being on the planet earth. And Shackleton gathers us together like the mother hen he is, and says to us, 'Ship and stores are gone, now we go home' … like it was just around the corner … But I am telling you, Shackleton, he meant it, he made a promise to us that morning that he etched on his heart: he would get us home.

From *Tom Crean – Antarctic Explorer* (Aidan Dooley)

Of the three expeditions Tom Crean made to the Antarctic, the third one, the *Endurance* expedition 1914–1916, was probably his most astounding achievement. The expedition, as it turned out, was aptly named. Shackleton's plan was to become the first to traverse the 1,800 miles across the Antarctic from coast to coast. They would approach the Antarctic from the South American side, make their way through the pack ice of the Weddell Sea, then a small group would land at Vahsel Bay and attempt to traverse the entire continent via the South Pole.

But, as Shackleton wrote in his diary, 'What the ice wants the ice gets.' And the treacherous Weddell Sea wanted his beautiful Norwegian ship. When the *Endurance* became stuck in the frozen sea, finally perishing in its icy grip, Shackleton and his men had to abandon all thoughts of their ambitious plan. Staying alive was now their only purpose. Stranded on the ice and with no rescue possible, the twenty-eight men were now locked in mortal combat against a fearsome enemy: the Antarctic weather. They were cast adrift on an open ice floe and with just five tents to protect them from the sub-zero temperatures, their hope was that they would eventually drift to the open sea where they would attempt to sail to safety. They miraculously managed to live for five months on a moving piece of ice that could, and did, crack at any moment. Somehow, they all managed to avoid plunging to their deaths.

Finally they reached the open sea and set sail: their three small lifeboats woefully inadequate to cope with the terrors of the turbulent Southern Ocean. Tom Crean was at the tiller of the smallest boat, a Norwegian cutter called *Stancomb Wills*. While some of the men in his boat were caving under the pressure, Crean was a calm, stoical presence throughout the hazardous journey. It was six days before the exhausted, frostbitten, battered men finally reached the dry land of Elephant Island. It was an inhospitable, uninhabited land that offered a valuable resting place, but safety was still a long way off. Realising that most of the men were not fit to attempt another open-boat journey, Shackleton decided that just six men would take the *James Caird* lifeboat and make the epic 800-mile trip to South Georgia to mobilise a rescue ship for the twenty-two men left behind on Elephant Island. Almost inevitably, trusted Tom Crean was one of them.

The odds were stacked against the success of their rescue attempt: what realistic chance did they have in their small open boat on the world's most dangerous seas? This was, no doubt, not something the six men dwelled on as they bade farewell to their comrades and launched their boat onto the thunderous waves. It was a bleak journey. Each of the six men suffered severe seasickness and had very little rest in their wet reindeer sleeping bags as the treacherous sea tossed the tiny vessel in its tumultuous swell. Once again, Crean was a cheery tower of strength and he would often sing (allegedly none too well) at the helm, which was both comfort and irritation to his fellow sailors. Miraculously, after around two and a half weeks in a 23-foot-long open boat, the severely weakened men reached South Georgia. They barely had enough strength to pull the boat on to the beach, but they were alive.

The rescue journey was not yet finished, however. For help lay on the other side of the island, at the whaling station, and with the boat no longer seaworthy, the only way to get there was to cross South Georgia on foot. No human being had ever done it before, let alone exhausted men with no proper equipment. The terrain was hostile to say the least, with a jagged, inhospitable mountain range to negotiate. It was an almost suicidal expedition but there was no choice: twenty-eight lives were depending on it. Shackleton would take two men with him: one was Frank Worsley, whose skills as a navigator would be crucial, and the other was Tom Crean, steadfast, unshakeable and strong in mind and body. Hope, courage and dogged determination would be needed on this journey into the unknown. Their trek was tortuous: for thirty-six hours they dragged themselves up and down mountains, with no sleep and with severe dehydration. At one point, Shackleton, Crean and Worsley had no choice but to sit on their behinds and slide at around 60 mph down a mountain in the dark, knowing that meeting a rock or crevasse would mean certain death. By yet another miracle, they once again survived and made it, at last, to the whaling station. One hardy Norwegian whaler wept at the sight of the three ragged, spent men who staggered into the station, their heroic rescue mission nearly ended. When a relief ship finally arrived at Elephant Island, all twenty-two men were still alive.

The *Endurance* expedition is, by any standard, an incredible, triumphant tale of survival against all the odds. And at the time I first started performing my show, very few people understood Tom Crean's pivotal role in Shackleton's famously death-defying journey. It is, however, an epic tale and I feared it was too long to dramatise fully in all its glory during my short play. For that reason, I hadn't included it in that first performance on Irish soil in autumn 2001, concentrating instead on the Scott expeditions, particularly the *Terra Nova*, which I knew best.

So, there I was after the Tralee show, looking at a sea of raised arms as the entire audience confirmed they would be coming to see me for a second time the following night at the South Pole Inn. I felt obliged to give them something different: surely I owed them that? Looking back, I can see that I could have just done the same thing again but I thought the audience would be bored, that I wouldn't be able to hold their attention again if I did the same material. There was nothing for it, I reasoned, but to do the *Endurance* expedition. I had done little bits of the story back in London at the museum but I was by no means familiar with it. Throughout the remainder of that night and the next day, I spent most of my time thinking about how I was going to change the show for the following performance. I didn't get much sleep that night.

It was, in all sorts of ways, an unforgettable weekend in Kerry. The next day, Saturday, we went to Annascaul and I visited some of the nearby places that played such a significant part in Tom's life. I went to Minard Castle with its extraordinary beach of huge rounded boulders, where Tom ran off to join the Royal Navy, aged fifteen, in July 1883 after an (alleged) argument with his father. I was incredibly moved to visit Tom's burial site, which is a mile or so outside the village, and to see the mini mausoleum where he is interred with his wife, Ellen, and daughter Katie, who had died at the age of four after an epileptic fit. And I climbed up the mountains above Annascaul, to the corrie lake, called the Black Lake because it is so deep that the waters look darkly fathomless. It was here that retired Tom and his beloved dogs would walk in splendid isolation for hours on end, no doubt reflecting on his time in the mountains of the Antarctic.

And then there was Tom's home, the South Pole Inn, where I was to perform the show. He bought the pub for his retirement but never actually worked in it, leaving all of that to his wife, Ellen. Tom didn't like to talk about his time in the Antarctic. His daughters Mary and Eileen told me he kept his medals, including his prized Albert Medal and official medals marking his three voyages to the Antarctic, hidden away in a box and that almost everything they learned about his heroic efforts was after his death. But at least the name of his pub, incongruous against the green Kerry countryside, pays tribute to his glory days as an explorer.

I was to perform in a room above the bar. In Tom's day, the upstairs had three rooms where the family would have lived, but they had now been knocked through into one big room. I decided to put myself in one corner, in what used to be Tom's bedroom, a decision, as it turns out, that would have a profound effect on me. Mary and Eileen had told their children and grandchildren about the

Aidan performing the second half of the play for the first time, in Tom Crean's former bedroom above the South Pole Inn, October 2001.

show, so there were to be around twenty of Tom's descendants in the audience, along with my parents and the audience from the night before, plus some curious locals. I had spent the previous night and the whole day cogitating about how I would change the show to include the Shackleton story. But, as I waited in the storeroom, preparing to meet my audience, I still was not sure what would come out of my mouth once I began.

The room was packed, with around fifty or so people. And out I went on to the 'stage', on my second Antarctic journey that weekend, this time including the story of Shackleton and the *Endurance* expedition. It all seemed to be going well, the audience was rapt and I was getting towards the end of the show when something very strange happened. In character as Tom, I was explaining how I had bought the pub for my retirement and wanted to call it the South Pole in tribute to the place that had been such a big part of my life. In the script, Tom is imagining his new job as a publican when he says: 'Wouldn't it be magnificent to be upstairs with my wife and two living daughters, putting my collar and tie on to go to work below at the South Pole?' I started saying this line and then I stopped abruptly mid-sentence. I was suddenly struck by the thought that, here I was, performing in his former bedroom, a place he had inhabited for so many years, standing on the same floor, with the same fireplace and walls. I felt overcome. It's difficult to explain without sounding mad, but for a few seconds everything stood still, everything was wiped out and it was just me and Tom Crean. It was as though this strong presence of Tom came right into me, that he had somehow given me his permission to get inside his skin and do my show.

Hero of the Antartic is recalled as play is staged in his bedroom

By Alden Corkery

THE CLOCK was turned back and an eerie quiet descended around the upstairs of the South Pole Inn in Annascaul last Saturday as a one man play recounting the life of Antarctic explorer Tom Crean was performed in his former bedroom before his two daughters.

The piece, which forms part of an Antarctic exhibition at the National Maritime Museum in London, was the highlight of a weekend which also included a visit to Crean's grave in Ballinacourty and a lecture on Antarctic exploration by the curator of the National Maritime Museum exhibition, Sian Flynn.

The previous night the biographical piece was also performed at Siamsa Tíre, where it received an eager recep-tion from those who attended.

Speaking about the Annascaul perfor-mance, Kerry County Museum curator Helen O'Carroll said that it was fascinating to see the story of Crean's life being retold before his two daughters Mary and Eileen O'Brien.

"He told the piece in Tom Crean's old room, upstairs in the South Pole Inn," explained Ms O'Carroll. "It was almost as if you had gone back in time to see his daughters there lis-tening to it in front of him."

The visit by members of the British National Maritime Museum coin-cides with the ongoing plans by Kerry County Museum to establish an exhibition of Tom Crean memorabilia, commem-orating the central role he played in the Antarctic exhibitions of both Earnest Scott and Sir Earnest Shackleton.

As the museum's cura-tor, Ms Carroll admitted it was wonderful to be able to consult with offi-cials from as prestigious a museum as the British National Maritime Museum and added that their experience of host-ing an Antarctic exhibi-tion would prove invalu-able to her own museum's efforts.

Born in 1877, Tom Crean joined the Navy at the age of 15 and became a key member of three of the four major British expeditions of the first two decades of the twen-tieth century.

During his later life, 'Tom the Pole' as he was known to his neigh-bours, never spoke of his experiences in the Antarctic and his role for many years until the publication of his biog-raphy last year.

Actor Aidan Dooley dressed as Tom Crean on Elephant Island in the Antartic during a performance of the show at Siamsa Tíre, Tralee.   Pic: McMonagle

The *Kerryman* review of the play's performance in the South Pole Inn, October 2001.

And as I was having this strange, surreal, spiritual, special moment, I was also aware that there were fifty or so faces turned towards me expectantly. I had stopped mid-sentence. I'm not honestly sure what I said at that point to the audience, something like 'this is very strange', but I managed to back up and start the line again.

When I talked to them later, the audience said they had also been aware of something oddly intense going on. Had I been touched by the spirit of Tom, or was it me simply feeling emotional at being in his space, in his very home? I couldn't really say, but it was unforgettable and exhilarating. I also was thrilled that the audience loved the show. An American woman in the question-and-answer session afterwards said to me, 'Are you Tom?' The transatlantic translation (I think) is that she was asking if I became so caught up in the moment that I forgot who I was. I said to her, 'Oh no, I'm never Tom. I inhabit him for a while, but I'm always Aidan Dooley playing Tom Crean.' To believe anything else would be madness, or pretentious at the very least. Even so, after that vivid moment in the South Pole pub, I felt I now carried a little bit of Tom inside me.

3
ON THE TRAIL OF ADVENTURE

I wasn't in the army: I joined the Royal Navy, and I joined the Royal Navy a year afore I was supposed to join. I was only fifteen. I joined because of where I'm from – I never thought of that …

From *Tom Crean – Antarctic Explorer* (Aidan Dooley)

Nestled quietly among the hills of the Irish-speaking Dingle Peninsula is Annascaul, a small village that would have remained hidden off the beaten track but for the adventures of its local hero. Nowadays, visitors make a special detour to come and see the place where Tom Crean was born and where he was finally laid to rest. Just outside the village still stands the farmhouse where

Tom spent the first fifteen years of his life. A few years ago, I was lucky enough to stay there at the invitation of Tom's grandson Enda who now owns it. What a thrill it was for me to step over the threshold of Tom's family home, to picture him at the kitchen table and to look out onto the land that his father had worked. Although it is not far from the village itself, the house is surrounded by fields and feels quite remote. We stayed at the house during an icy December. It was freezing cold both inside and out and the nights were ferociously black. I was struck by the isolation of the place and it was not hard to imagine that a young man growing up in this rural community in the late 1870s might dream of a world beyond.

It was a memorable few days in Annascaul. Enda had invited myself, my wife Miriam and our two children, Liam and Nancy, to watch the pipe band of New York's fire brigade bring in the new year. It's a fantastic new tradition that sees a torchlit procession through the village. It is quite a sight to behold as the gathered crowd hold aloft their flaming turfs on the end of pikes, led along the village road at midnight by the rousing tunes of the pipe band who fly over from America especially for the occasion. Two or three years before our visit there had apparently been more drama than anticipated when one of the lit torches fell under a car. Ironically, the good firefighters of New York couldn't help as they were busy playing their pipes. The looming disaster was averted when half a dozen local men simply lifted up the car and retrieved the torch. Always handy to have a big, strong Kerry farmer in a crisis, as Scott and Shackleton discovered.

Not that Tom Crean was destined to be a farmer like his father. Young Thomas had seen first-hand the difficulties of living off the land. He was born in 1877, when the spectre of the Great Famine of 1845–1852 was still hovering and threatening to blight the potato crops once again. Tom was one of ten children – six boys and four girls – and, with so many mouths to feed, life must have been a constant struggle for Patrick Crean and his wife, Catherine. Though he was not the oldest son, who would traditionally take over the farm, Tom was a strong lad, made tougher by a childhood where food, money and parental attention were in short supply. So he was no doubt expected to provide strong support in the running of the farm. Young Tom, however, was having none of it. His dreams and ambitions lay in distant horizons, away from this insular world. And so, in the best tradition of young adventurers, he took the only obvious escape route open to him and ran away to sea.

The circumstances of Tom joining the Royal Navy are anecdotal but the tale that has been handed down through Crean family folklore is that he ran away to sea after an argument with his father. The story goes that Tom had been entrusted with tending the cows and accidentally let them get into the bottom field where, overnight, they proceeded to eat the all-important potato crop. Given that Tom's father had lived through the first potato famine, you could imagine that he did not take too well to the careless loss of their precious crop. No doubt with his father's angry words still fresh in his mind, fifteen-year-old Tom made his way to Minard Castle where the Royal Navy were recruiting. Somehow – and again, we don't really know how – the navy representative was persuaded to accept this youthful recruit, who was underage by one year. Perhaps he had a forged certificate, maybe he lied about his date of birth, or perhaps they recognised a certain flinty fearlessness in this Kerry lad and chose to overlook the little matter of his age. Either way, within two weeks he had said goodbye to his family, borrowed a suit, and made his way to Cobh where, on 10 July 1893, Thomas Crean became Boy 2nd Class in the Royal Navy.

According to a writer I met, who had been researching Tom's naval life, his earlier years prior

The St Columcille United Gaelic Pipe Band from New York City in Annascaul on New Year's Eve, 2008.

to the polar trips were full of ups and downs. He would do well enough to climb up to Petty Officer and would then mysteriously be knocked back down to Able Seaman. The navy listings gave no explanation for this, but the writer said it is likely to have been as a reaction to Tom fighting or getting drunk while ashore. Although well suited to a navy career, this tendency to get into trouble must have held Tom back in those early days. But that all changed with the good ship *Discovery*.

In August 1901 the *Discovery* left the Isle of Wight on the first leg of its journey to the Antarctic. I can imagine that such a historic voyage generated as much publicity and hype as the moon landings less than seventy years later. Crean was not part of Robert Falcon Scott's original crew and it was four months later, in Lyttelton Harbour in New Zealand, when Tom first stepped aboard. At the time he was a crew member on HMS *Ringarooma*, a cruiser moored next to the *Discovery* at Lyttleton. The captain of the *Ringarooma* had been asked by the Admiralty to make his crew available to help prepare the *Discovery* for her epic trip. As Tom helped mend the rigging, fix leaks and overhaul the vessel, would he have been wishing that he, too, would be setting sail to the ends of the earth on this most epic of expeditions?

The ruin of the sixteenth-century Minard Castle, built by the Fitzgeralds. The Royal Navy had a recruiting office nearby, where Tom Crean enlisted. MICHAEL DIGGIN

It was a twist of fate that gave Tom his ticket to ride. One of Scott's signed-up crew, an unpopular troublemaker called Harry J. Baker, deserted after striking an officer, leaving the *Discovery* expedition one man short. The anecdotal story goes (but there is no reason not to believe it) that Tom volunteered to fill the vacancy and on 10 December 1901 Able Seaman Crean signed up to the expedition. But the

41

very first step on his Antarctic journey was tinged with tragedy. On 21 December, as the *Discovery* prepared to set sail from Lyttelton Harbour, the cheering crowd on the quay were suddenly silenced by a fatal accident. Charles Bonner, a young crew member from London's East End, had climbed up the *Discovery*'s mainmast in celebratory mood, probably fuelled by the alcohol he had consumed, and fell to his death. Not the most auspicious start to any voyage but for Tom it was the start of a polar career, the chance for an ordinary seaman to become an extraordinary hero. The real adventures had begun.

A century later, I made my own escape from the ordinary. I hesitate to draw any parallels between Tom's career and mine, but we are at least alike in refusing to conform to the life that was seemingly mapped out for us. We both flouted our family's expectations in order to seek something 'other', something different and more exciting. While Tom escaped the confines of rural Ireland to sail the seas and conquer continents, I managed to break free of my job at Allied Irish Bank to become, well, an actor. Yes, I know it doesn't quite have the same heroic ring to it but choosing to leave a secure career for the vagaries of acting was risky in its own way, believe me, especially in 1987 when many Irish

Aidan's father, Jimmy Dooley, photographed at a Sunday morning jazz gig when he was in his eighties.

were struggling to find work. My parents certainly thought so. It was just something I had to do.

I never had a hankering to be an actor when I was young and had no family pathway into that world. I grew up happily in Galway with four sisters and two brothers, all older than me. If anything, my family's performing talents were musical. My paternal grandfather, Michael, played the fiddle and was also in a brass band in Galway called St

Patrick's Brass Band. According to my father, his dad came back one night from playing in the band and said 'Jaysus, there was a man there tonight playing the saxophone and they gave him 10 bob for it. Ten bob!' So the next day my grandfather goes out and buys a saxophone and drives the whole street mad learning to play it. Then he had an idea that he would start one of these Glenn Miller type bands with my father, Jimmy, on drums, and his older brother, Maxie, as accordian/piano player. I still have a fantastic photo of this band (see p. 45), called The Arabians, which toured around dance halls and community halls in the west of Ireland on Saturday and Sunday nights. My grandfather was a blacksmith by trade and playing music was a way of making a few extra pounds. As the band's popularity grew, my other uncles, Christy and Cyril, joined and it became a full family affair.

After my grandfather died suddenly at fifty-two, my dad's oldest brother, Maxie, took over the running of The Arabians. My father stayed in it for ten years, but he always had a full-time job and the band money supplemented his income. He was conscious that he had to earn enough to feed his family, a sense of responsibility that I inherited from him. We Dooleys are, I suppose, a pragmatic bunch.

Aidan's father Jimmy Dooley's band, The Arabians, pictured in the 1950s. In the back row are Jimmy (*left*) and Aidan's uncles Kieran (*centre*) and Cyril (*right*).

Despite my best efforts, I was not cut out for music. I joined a brass band at the age of ten but I didn't have any talent for it. I joined because my dad played music, as did my brothers Raymond and Gerard. I never remember my dad actually listening to music very often, perhaps because the record player was dominated by my sisters. He obviously had a knack for music, however, and taught himself to play the drums. But my brothers, who are fifteen and thirteen years older than me, always loved music and they were very cool because they were in bands and gigged.

Gerard played in Galway's pubs as a solo singing act and my eldest brother, Raymond, played bass in a band called The Archway, which performed at the Oslo Hotel and The Hangar in Salthill, amongst others. They had dreams of stardom and I don't suppose they were short of groupies. I, on the other hand, did not quite make the grade as a cool musician. I was second cornet for many years and all I ever played was the same couple of notes: 'de de de de de de daa!' I never actually played the melody. I remember once my uncle Christie inviting me up to play at a popular jazz session they did every Sunday in Galway and I had to say no because I was terrified that I would be found out. I didn't do tunes, I just did 'de de daa!'

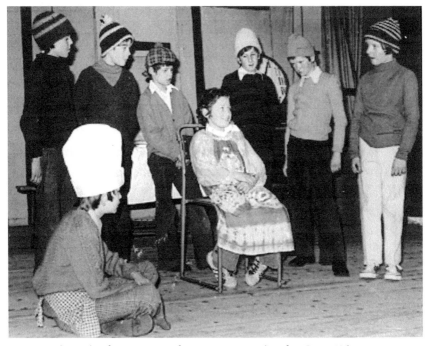

Aidan in his first stage performance – as a dwarf in *Snow White* (*second from right*) – while in fifth class at St Pat's National School.

Acting was another matter. I didn't exactly have an early yearning for the stage. My first experience of being on stage was singing 'Yellow Bird' in the Claddagh Hall in Galway. I must have been five or six years old and it was one of those community events that goes on and on. All I remember of that night is waiting for what seemed an eternity before it was our turn to perform. My first significant role was at secondary school. I went to 'the Bish', as we called St Joseph's College, and once a year teachers Mr Ferguson and Mr Breathnach produced a school show. My first one was a musical version of *Nicholas Nickleby* called *Smike*. I shared the lead role with my friend Donal O'Brien – we would do alternate nights – and I was a bit peeved because he sang for three nights and I sang for only two. But something really clicked for me during that show. I loved it. My voice may not have been as good as Donal's but everyone was telling me I acted the part much better than he did. It dawned on me that I might really be able to act. Suddenly, I was no longer a nobody in the playground and it felt amazing. But I didn't have much chance to pursue this new-found talent beyond a couple of further school productions. At that time in Ireland there wasn't a drama club you could join. The nearest thing to it were elocution classes, which my sisters attended. I was too young to go and, anyway, I was a boy so I wouldn't be needing them. That was the thinking, at any rate.

When I left school I didn't have good enough results in my Leaving Certificate to go to university. Not that I wanted to go. I was pleased that I no longer had the pressure of having to learn things. If it hadn't been for my mother I might, like Tom, have become a member of the armed forces. In my final

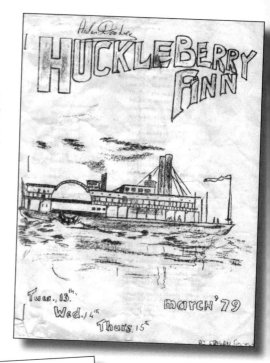

The programme from Aidan's fifth-year play in secondary school, *Huckleberry Finn*, 1979.

C A S T

Aunt Polly	Dympna O'Byrne
Mrs Harper	Sarah Halliday
Mrs Temple	Derval Byrne
Mary	Marian Hayden
Jones	Ciaran Connell
Ned	Donal O Brien
Judge Thatcher	Donnchadh O Madagain
Muff Potter	Michael Biblin
Sheriff	Aidan Dooley
Injun Joe	Niall Rabbitt
Prosecutor	Paul Canavan
Doc Robinson	Noel Furey
Jim (. .)	Gerry Ferguson
	Ger O'Halloran
Other Voices	Peadar O'Grady / Kevin Munroe
Huck	Robert Craine / Ruairi Fahy
Tom	Paul Heaney
Sid	Tom Lennon
Ben Rogers	Frank Costello
Joe Harper	John Flannelly
Alfred Temple	Mary Curran, Bernie Deacy,
Female Chorus	Helen Ryan, Imelda Cosgrave,
	Lorraine Wright, Ruth Cunningham
	Valerie Langan, Una Foyle,
	Margaret Joyce
Male Chorus	Padraic McDonnell, Padraic Glynn
Male Chorus	Padraic Talbot, Brendan Ray,
	Damien Byrne, Michael Jacob,
	David Kelly, Michael Wall
	Peter Heffernan, Mark O'Toole,
	Gerard Coughlan, Eric Maye.
	Timothy McWilliams, Shane Fahy,
	Thomas Cox, Jimmy Cahill,
	Con Crowley, Dermot Nolan,
	John Kelly, Kevin Keogh,
	Ciaran McMahon.

two years in school I joined the army. Well, okay, it wasn't the real army: it was the reserve army, the FCA, the Irish version of the volunteer Home Guard. But we wore berets with badges and long coats, learned how to drill and fire weapons, and I was good at it. In the summer you went away to camp for two weeks, when you were paid the same as a real army soldier (it was part of the numbers game for the Irish Government who, as part of the European Union, had made an obligation to have a certain number of trained personnel) and learned how to fire fifty-year-old guns from the Second World War. I enjoyed all this and probably could have progressed to a job in the army but for my mother. She had other plans for my future. Without my knowledge, she filled in an application form for the Allied Irish Bank on my behalf, and I was offered a job. (For the first two years at the bank I never used my own signature but tried to sign my name like my mother had, just in case our guilty secret was discovered.)

I had never set my sights on a career in the bank despite being good with numbers. But like Tom's navy career, it was a good, secure job, a job for life. They would buy your coffin for you. So when I was offered a full-time position with Allied Irish, I was pleased, not least because it meant that for the first time I was standing on my own two feet. In October 1980, I left Galway to start my new life in Dublin. My father drove me to the train station in the Ford Cortina I had washed every Saturday (oh yes, I worked for that pocket money). He sent me off with one brief piece of advice: 'Trust no one' which, looking back, was my dad's way of saying 'Take care of yourself.'

But nothing could dampen my excitement at being in Dublin. When I arrived, in my good clothes, to join the other recruits on the first day, we were each given an envelope that would decide our fate. Inside was the name of the branch to which we had been assigned and which could have been anywhere in Ireland. I could have found myself in deepest Cork or, heaven forbid, in a one-horse town with no rail link to Galway and so have found it impossible to get home regularly. But by sheer fluke I landed 100 Grafton Street. O happy day!

There I was, a seventeen-year-old in Dublin, sharing a flat with my school friend Mike Higgins and meeting lots of other young people, earning good money, out drinking most nights and having a great time. After a couple of years I eventually got involved in a couple of drama groups, which became a really important part of my life. One of these was The Mercury Players, which I joined after answering a newspaper advertisement for members. This group took itself quite seriously. I performed with them in play after play and made some wonderful friends, most notably my great pal John Morgan, who recognised and encouraged an acting potential in me from the start. The group was on the amateur-dramatic festival circuit. I remember my grandmother coming to see me in Galway where I played Algernon in *The Importance of Being Earnest*. She said to me afterwards, 'I didn't understand a word you were saying but you looked splendid.'

All our performances at the festivals were critiqued by adjudicators in order to improve our acting. Some weren't too tough on us amateurs (though they might question whether the glamorous make-up was really quite appropriate, Mary, since you were playing a Famine victim …) but others were needlessly ruthless and vindictive. Critics notwithstanding, I loved being on stage. I was once told that, although I had a tendency to rabbit and no technique to speak of, I had something more: I had imagination. My head started to fill with notions …

But if the stage felt like the natural place for me to be, I started to feel like an outsider at the bank. As the years went on, I became more disillusioned with it. I hated the mundanity of it, doing the same thing

The programme for the Mercury Players' production of *The Importance of Being Earnest*, 1984.

MERCURY PLAYERS

"THE IMPORTANCE OF BEING ERNEST"

by Oscar Wilde.

Character:	Played by:
John Worthing, J.P.	John Morgan
Algernon Moncrieff	Aidan Dooley
Lady Bracknell	Betty Clandillon
Hon. Gwendolen Fairfax	Margaret Hannigan
Cecily Cardew	Lynda Cullen
Miss Prism (Governess)	Peggie Cahill
Rev. Canon Chasuble, D.D.	Declan Fahy
Lane (Manservant)	Fergus Madden
Merriman (Butler)	Vivian Dillon

Producer	Jenny Murphy
Stage Management	Mairead Allen / Kevin Collins
Lighting	Vivian Dillon

Act I: Algernon Moncrieff's flat in Half-Moon Street, London W.

Act II: The garden at the Manor House, Woolton.

Act III: Drawing-room at the Manor House, Woolton.

Time: 1895

Intervals: Two fifteen minute intervals.

day in, day out. I used to like being on the counter, being sociable and chatting to customers, but then I was sent backstage to the computer department and every day I would be robotically filling in dockets, punching in numbers and logging credits. To relieve the monotony I would start discussions with fellow workers, such as 'Why do men have nipples?' or 'Why is there salt in the sea?' I was known as a bit of a lunatic, the joker. What I was, I suppose, was a square peg in a round hole. I was good at my job, though, and fast. If you got through all the dockets, you were able to leave work early and go home. In my case, home was above the shop, as I was living rent-free in the bank flat because they liked to have someone in the premises at night. So my ambition every day became about being back in my flat by 4.15 p.m. to watch *The Smurfs* on TV.

There was no question of me leaving the bank. What would I do? It was all very well loving the acting but there was no such thing as full-time professional training in Ireland in 1982. I was a 21-year-old with a job for life; the idea of becoming an actor was simply an impossibility. Or maybe not. It occurred to me that if I got a transfer to an Allied Irish branch in England, then maybe some acting possibilities might open up and perhaps I could pursue some acting training across the water.

So I put in for a transfer, only to be told that England was no longer recruiting from Ireland. And that could have been that, but one day, months later, I was approached by Mr Joyce, the dapper bowler-hatted bank manager who had been our boss since the beginning. I remember vividly seeing his bird-like frame silhouetted against the wall as he asked me, out of the blue, in his posh Dublin accent: 'Do you still want to go to England?' And that was it, one of those slow-motion moments when you know that your decision could change your life forever.

It transpired that there had been a strike in England, which was now resolved, but part of the resolution meant addressing staff shortages by bringing in extra workers. And they wanted them as soon as possible. I asked Mr Joyce if I could think about it. He said 'of course' but gave me just fifteen minutes to make the biggest decision of my life. Should I leave everything and everyone I knew and go in search of what could turn out to be an impossible dream? I didn't know anyone in London. I had been there only once, when I was ten, and even then I got lost on the Tube. I didn't know anything about acting training in England. In any case, since I had first put in for the bank transfer, things had settled down for me and I had come to terms with the fact that I wasn't going to be an actor. It wasn't that I wanted to leave Ireland. I was quite happy with the Dublin scene. So I could stay – and then what? Probably marry within the bank, as most colleagues did, and then a bank mortgage and a bank car, and after that would come the bank babies and you'd be locked in forever. Ah yes, there it was. Lifelong, mundane security, with a coffin thrown in. Or the chance to step off the treadmill and take a leap into the unknown.

I took less than fifteen minutes to make up my mind. I didn't consult with anyone because I didn't think they would understand my dilemma. The answer was, as it has always been for me: I want to explore what's around the corner. I want the adventure.

Once I had said yes to the England transfer, I had just a week to prepare and say my goodbyes. On my last Friday at the bank I was looking forward to my leaving party in the evening. But at around 2 p.m. I received a phone call that made my blood run cold. An Irish voice was on the other end, a woman. She told me that she had been involved in the recent bank workers strike over in England and that, as a result of her being so vociferous in the dispute, the bank was victimising her and forcibly transferring her back to Ireland with her husband and two children. In short, I was being given her job. I could feel the blood drain from my face and I felt sick. I had been offered the chance at happiness, at a brand-new future and now it could be snatched away. How could I now step into this woman's shoes? The situation was testing all of my union ideologies. I just didn't know what to do so I asked if I could call her back.

I decided to seek advice from one manager I liked, a man from Cork, and luckily his door was open. So I knocked and went in. Just as I was about to launch into my problem, the phone rang. His face was unreadable as he listened to the caller but he didn't take his eyes off me. Afterwards, he said: 'Aidan, it's all been a wind-up. None of it is true.' My esteemed colleagues, led I believe, by Ken Creed, a friend to this day, had decided to play a trick on me and had asked one of their friends to phone me up. They had all been listening and watching as I took the call. They watched with amusement as my face paled and then with mild panic when I went in to the manager's office. They called him to explain and ask him to go along with the prank but he didn't have the heart to. I once told a friend this story and they thought it was a very cruel joke in bad taste, but I don't think they meant any malice. I mainly felt relieved that it wasn't true and I was able to laugh about it. In a strange way, it had been a sign of affection that my co-workers would have gone to so much trouble for me. And, crucially, the panic I had felt when I felt the new job slipping away from me reaffirmed just how much I wanted to go to England and see how far I could go with the acting.

And so it was that I packed all my worldly goods in a suitcase and left home for the second time to start working in London's Cricklewood branch of Allied Irish Bank. It took a while to get used to it. For a start, it was a much smaller branch than the Grafton Street branch and it had nothing like the ready-made social life I had enjoyed back home. To make matters worse, I had ruptured my knee playing football and, a year after arriving in London, had to have an operation. I'll never forget lying in the hospital bed the night before the operation, my knee as big as a watermelon. A guy came around with a marker pen and drew a big arrow on it. I said, 'Isn't it obvious which knee it is?' His reply was, 'You can never be too sure.' No one came to visit me during my week in hospital and I was going home to a flat I shared with five young bank guys, all of them working, so I couldn't expect much in the way of nursing care. On my first morning out of hospital I cried because I couldn't even put on my socks or make food. Luckily, my brother-in-law's sister Angela turned up, prompted by my Mam, I reckon, and whisked me away to her house in north London where she looked after me for weeks. She was my guardian angel then and I will remain close to her always.

It was Angela who gave me the push I needed to kick-start my acting dreams. Before the operation, I had been accepted onto a two-year part-time acting course at Morley College but because of my operation, I had missed the beginning of the course. I was just going to accept that I'd missed my opportunity, but Angela persuaded me to fight for my place, so I did. It was on the course at Morley over the following months that I began meeting the kind of people who had never been in my orbit before. What set them apart, perhaps, was that they believed that it is possible to choose happiness over security. They looked aghast when I told them about my unhappy job at the bank. 'What?' they exclaimed. 'You're going to stay in that job? What kind of eejit are you?' (Except being English, they might have actually said, 'Are you out of your mind?'). For six years I had been cocooned in this mentality that says you don't leave a job for life, even if you hate it.

So I was going to Cricklewood Allied Irish by day and immersing myself in acting at Morley College on Thursday and Friday nights and all day Saturday. Acting for a living still remained an elusive dream but at least I was getting my thespian fix. Life at the bank was pretty miserable but not without its own dramatic moments. We were held up at gunpoint one day. When the fella with a stocking over his head said, 'Down on the floor!' I put my physical acting training to good use and was down in a heartbeat. There were about six of us on the floor and none of us dared move or look around in case he was watching. He didn't get any money in the end because the bag he took was one of the dummy bags that bank security guys always carry. My line manager, who had, for some reason, taken a dislike to me, said afterwards: 'I've never seen Aidan Dooley move so fast as when he dropped to the ground.' He wasn't paying me a compliment.

I was so miserable at the bank I remember phoning home and crying to my Mam, who couldn't cope with my being upset and said, 'Talk to your Dad.' He said to me: 'I think what you have to do now, Aidan, is to decide you're going to make a go of this bank job and put out of your head these other dreams. Try it for four months and see if you can be happy, then if you can't, you know you will have given it your best shot.' And so I did. I tried my best to be happy with life at Allied Irish. But then came a pivotal moment that really made things clearer.

The assistant manager was gunning for me because he just didn't like it that I had another life outside work. He gave me an awful appraisal in which he made up things about me, saying that I had made mistakes when I hadn't. I went in to see his boss with the evidence that my appraisal was less than accurate. But the manager told me he wasn't able do anything about this because he couldn't undermine his assistant. What happened next is perhaps an inelegant expression of all those years of boredom and frustration. I headbutted the table, with a ferocity that sent the bank manager scuttling out of the room in fear that I would kill him. As a final nail in the coffin of my bank career, I refused to sign the fabricated appraisal.

Meantime, my acting course was going brilliantly. I reached another step nearer to my dreams when I was given the lead in the play *Whose Life Is It Anyway?* by Brian Clark. It's a terrific part about a man who's paralysed in a car accident and wants to be allowed to die. I took a week off from the bank and, with my script and my book of Stanislavsky, went on holiday to Jersey so I could immerse myself in it and prepare for the role. It was just after the Brighton bombing in October 1984, when the IRA bombed the Grand Hotel in Brighton where the Conservative Party conference was being held, in an attempt to kill the then British Prime Minister, Margaret Thatcher, and her Cabinet colleagues. Thatcher was uninjured but five people were killed and thirty-one were wounded. It took a day or two for me to realise why everyone was looking at me. Here was this Irishman, on his own, talking to no one … very suspicious indeed.

My Mam and sister Ursula came over to London to see me in the play and my teachers were full of praise for my performance. It was then that I actually thought, 'well, here is something.' Could I actually do this? I started auditioning for drama schools, was accepted by four and finally signed up for the postgraduate course at Guildford School of Acting.

All that remained was to break the news to my parents. Over in Galway, my mother was silent on the other end of phone. But she didn't try to convince me otherwise. I was no longer the young lad for whom she'd filled in the job application, I had moved on a lot. After those tear-filled phone calls, my leaving the bank wasn't exactly a bolt out of the blue. When I handed in my resignation – and bear in mind, this was a time when they were trying to dissuade people from leaving Allied Irish – the manager said to me: 'I think you'll be happier elsewhere.' I couldn't argue with that. I met him years later when he saw me in a show in the

West End and he asked me to talk to his son who, ironically enough, wanted to be an actor. He never mentioned the headbutting incident.

My decision to become an actor may have been ever so slightly more agonised than Tom's decision to enlist in the Royal Navy, but I got there in the end. I was at the bank for only seven years but now, over twenty-five years later, it remains an enormously vivid part of my life.

If the bank sometimes seemed like a prison, being at drama school felt like I'd died and gone to heaven. On my first day there in September 1987 I was like a kid in a sweet shop, not least because it was the first time I laid eyes on Miriam, a fellow student, in the mustard trousers and Doc Martens, with whom I would fall passionately in love and eventually marry. Romance aside, it was an enormously fruitful time for me. After years of being a round peg in a square hole I had, at last, found the perfect fit.

4
A LEAP OF FAITH

'What are we to do, sir?'

'We will strap ourselves onto the sledge and slide down the cliff.'

'I am not doing that.'

'You will do as you are told, Crean.'

'I won't …'

'You will.'

'Won't.'

'Will.'

It went on a few minutes, reminded me of my father before. Eventually I said, 'If Captain Scott was here, he wouldn't make us do that.' The officer, all 5ft 7 of him, stood up as tall as he could and looked up at me like that and said, 'Captain Scott isn't here.' He had dangly bits after all …

From *Tom Crean – Antarctic Explorer* (Aidan Dooley)

On the ice, when the ground beneath you can collapse at any second, every step you take could be your last. Decisions are life and death, actions are do or die, any error – a foot in the wrong place, a step in the wrong direction – can be fatal. Tom Crean, William Lashly and Lieutenant Teddy Evans were only too aware of this as they made their weary way back to Hut Point, having left Scott and his party to push on to the South Pole on 4 January 1912. If the harsh Antarctic weather weren't challenging enough, the trio was trying to negotiate the cryptic terrain without proper navigational tools, having given up their precious sledge meter to Scott's party. It is hardly surprising that the exhausted navigator, Lieutenant Evans, lost his bearings and eventually made the horrific discovery that they had veered miles off course. Faced with a possible three-day detour, which might cost them their lives, Evans came up with an audacious plan: the three men would strap themselves onto the sledge and free fall down 2,000 feet of sheer ice onto the mighty Beardmore Glacier below.

Tom Crean might not have embraced the prospect of plunging down the crevasse-strewn ice face into oblivion but the alternative was to take a longer, less spectacularly dangerous route and risk running out of food and energy. The men were stuck between the proverbial rock and hard place; both involved the very real possibility of an unhappy outcome. Being the kind of fella who was quick to volunteer himself when others might have held back, you would imagine that Tom would not want to wait for death to creep slowly on him, but would much prefer to square up to the Grim Reaper with a high-risk, death-defying sledge ride. So it was, that after a slight protest, he climbed aboard the humble chariot with comrades Evans and Lashly and they began their perilous descent. Flying along at 60 mph, they had no brakes and no protection. Somehow, the three avoided falling into the abundant, yawning crevasses and did not sustain any injuries more serious than cuts and bruises. Their hair-raising toboggan ride was the desperate act of men with few options and their survival was nothing short of miraculous. As Tom no doubt thanked God or counted his lucky stars that he was still in one piece, little did he know that four years later he would be taking another ride down another suicidally sheer ice face, this time with Ernest Shackleton and Frank Worsley during their legendary crossing of South Georgia. And this time he wouldn't even have a real sledge, but a makeshift toboggan-cum-mat fashioned out of rope.

It's fair to say that Tom's entire Antarctic career began with a similarly courageous leap into the unknown. He could not have had any real idea of what was to come when he signed up to join the *Discovery* that December in 1901. Legend has it (probably fictitiously) that when Shackleton was recruiting for crew for his *Endurance* expedition, he placed an advertisement in a newspaper that read: 'Men wanted for Hazardous Journey. Small wages, bitter cold, long months of complete darkness, constant danger, safe return doubtful. Honour and recognition in case of success.' Fictitious or not, the advert sums up both the risk and the accolades attached to a polar trip a century ago. For Tom, with no polar experience and no doubt that the *Discovery* voyage ahead was exceedingly dangerous, he was sailing into uncharted territory and was committed to Captain Scott's expedition for at least two years. A leap of faith indeed.

Tom's courage has been the heart of my show. His lionheart, his physical and mental strength, is what makes his legacy so extraordinary and why audiences have been so captivated by it. I recognised the power of his story from the beginning. After that momentous autumn weekend in Kerry in 2001 when I first brought the show to Ireland, I realised that, even in its half-formed state, I had the kernel of a potentially powerful piece of drama. So when I went back home to Galway the following summer, maybe this belief was what led me into the Taibhdhearc, a beautiful little theatre down a side street in the city centre. I spoke to the manager there about the possibility of performing my show. She had never heard of Tom Crean, but yes, they did have dates available, so I arranged to rent the theatre for two nights in late October. Bearing in mind that the show was only half formed, I didn't have anything resembling a script and only had the briefest acquaintance with the second act, this was my own leap of faith. As an added pressure, I was having to lay out money to rent the theatre with no idea if anyone would even turn up. And while I was away I was losing income from my museum work over in England, money that I could ill afford to lose at that point in my life.

But I believed in Tom's story and, as they say, fortune favours the bold. So with the Galway venue as a starting point, I decided to see if I could attract any other takers. I started phoning around – no Internet in those days – and by some stroke of good fortune spoke to Joe Murphy, who runs a small theatre in Listowel. He didn't know me from Adam and I will be forever grateful to Joe for agreeing to take the show. He booked it for one night after my

Galway dates. There was no rental cost: we would simply split the takings from the box office, 60–40 in my favour, and he'd throw in accommodation, too. I called the South Pole Inn in Annascaul to see if they wanted me to come back with Tom for a night. They did. I had also been invited to perform at the second-ever Athy Shackleton School, which is a weekend of lectures given and attended by polar experts and enthusiasts. So there it was: four venues on my first little tour. Right, then, I'd better finish the play …

A couple of months later, just before Christmas 2002, back I came to Ireland with a firmer idea of the play's structure. I still had no script; I just kept it all in my head. If I'd had a brain seizure, there would have been no record of the show. First stop Athy, Shackleton's place of birth and an audience that frankly scared the bejaysus out of me. I knew that the Athy School would be full of Antarctic experts and dedicated Shackleton enthusiasts, including his granddaughter, Lady Alexandra Shackleton, and three of his great-nephews. In the show I talked with great confidence about this speed or that height, or this and that polar fact. If I had got any detail wrong, they would know. My play was based on fact, but also supposition and was laced with a big dollop of my personality. Would these Shackleton devotees grant me artistic licence? I was on at 9 p.m. after dinner. During the performance I managed to keep my nerves under control but every time I saw an audience member whispering to their neighbour, my paranoia told me that they were remarking on something I'd got wrong. I feared they would tear me apart in the question-and-answer session afterwards. But it was quite the reverse. If there were any inaccuracies, the audience were far too gracious or polite to mention them. The overall response was gratifyingly positive. These experts were used to reading about the mighty Antarctic explorers, not seeing them brought to life through drama. They said they were deeply touched, that the play had given them an insight into the humanity of those famous explorers and it had been a very emotional experience. I set off for Galway with a little boost of confidence.

After the scary Athy audience, my home crowd would at least be familiar. Many of them would also be related to me. Unbeknown to me, my mother had swung into action and had become my publicist/ ticket booker. She had phoned around everyone we knew and had sold out the shows, filling the 150 seats on both nights. When I got to Galway she was the hub, the centre of activity. 'Bring these two tickets, now, up to Maureen,' she would say to my nephew while consulting the special book in which she had a record of everyone who was coming and when.

Aidan's parents, Jimmy and Ellen Dooley, in 2007.

My mother had also written to Galway Bay FM, the local radio station, and arranged an interview (live on air) with Keith Finnigan, a radio presenter and a former classmate of mine. Keith called me on my mobile as I was driving up to Holyhead to get the ferry and I pulled over into a service station to chat to him. Keith was chuckling away as he imagined me doing a show that had come from a museum, with my set (basically a sledge and a tarpaulin) packed into the back of my silver Ford Mondeo and my mother acting as my manager. I didn't mind his teasing. 'Ah well, necessity creates the best form of art,' was my pithy comment.

Looking back, those Galway performances were seat-of-the-pants stuff. It was a huge deal that I was doing the show in my home town in front of 300 people who were, thanks to my mother, a glorified extension of my family. They had come, out of loyalty or curiosity, to see Jimmy's young fella, Nelly's son, the one who had gone over to England to do the acting, given up his job at the bank and all. I felt as though there was a lot riding on it. Yet, even with the recent performance at Athy, I still barely knew the show, especially the second half. I arrived at the theatre and there was no technician. There was an odd jobs/caretaker, called Johnny I think, who knew my father and uncles and fixed the boiler at the theatre. He said, 'Do you want lights, Aidan?

AIDAN DOOLEY
AS

TOM CREAN
"ANTARCTIC EXPLORER"

*"A remarkable reproduction
of a remarkable man"*
Michael Smith, biographer 'Unsung Hero'

DIRECT FROM THE ACCLAIMED EXHIBITION "SOUTH" AT THE NATIONAL MARITIME MUSEUM GREENWICH

Athy Heritage Centre – Saturday 26th October 2002 – 0507 33075
Taibhdhearc Theatre, Galway – Monday 28th & Tuesday 29th October 2002 – 091 563600
South Pole Inn, Annascaul – Thursday 31st October 2002 – 066 9157382
St. Johns Theatre – Listowel – Friday 1st November 2002 – 068 22566

IN ASSOCIATION WITH SPECTRUM THEATRE PROJECTS

A flyer for Aidan's first tour.

C'mon, I'll show you where you push the buttons.'
My nephews Anthony and Brian had kindly offered
to help out. They had never done it before but, then
again, there weren't many lights to manage. There
was a problem with the heating, said Johnny, but
I was too distracted to take any notice of what he
said. The dressing room had that damp feeling that
is familiar to any actor who has done any small-
scale touring. Not that I was going to spend much
time in there. More importantly, the theatre itself is
a beautiful little space.

I started the show as I did in the museum, out
among the audience in the auditorium, chatting
to them as I pared down Tom's tobacco. It helped
to break down formality and also quelled my
nerves that night, so that by the time I started the
performance I didn't feel any fear. All was going
well until about halfway through the first act
when people started standing up to put on their
coats. Naturally I assumed they were all about to
leave having been thoroughly bored, unimpressed,
disengaged and all those other gloomy Dooley
predictions. 'Just keep going, Aidan' I urged myself,
trying to ignore this imminent mass exodus. If only
I'd been listening to Johnny earlier, I could have
saved myself a lot of angst. It turned out that the
heating was broken and everyone was freezing

cold. Having not walked out, the audience gave me and the show a rousing standing ovation and also stayed behind for a question-and-answer session.

If I'm being honest, I was so pumped up with adrenaline that night that the performance had passed in a bit of a blur. It was only when my brother raised his hand and asked the question, 'Aidan, what happened to the two lads in the tent?' that I realised, with horror, I had missed out a crucial part of the *Terra Nova* story. I had recounted Tom Crean's legendary solo march to get help, against all the odds, for the dying Lieutenant Evans and Bill Lashly, but I had not included the part where the pair are actually rescued. I simply forgot. That's the trouble when you are the lone actor as well as writer and director: you have no one to rely on but yourself and sometimes you get it wrong. Mistakes can be very helpful because they highlight something that could be made better, but sometimes it's just a one-off that you put down to nerves or tiredness, or a brief lack of concentration. You just have to forgive yourself and move on.

It was on the second night at Galway, during the post-show discussion, that I learned a very valuable lesson. A man put up his hand and said, 'I'm sure Tom Crean was no more than a British donkey. He was no more than some brawn for the British.' I suppose this sort of comment, laced with nationalist undertones, was part of the reason why Tom Crean stories were not abundant years earlier. It was the sort of attitude that I would hope my show could help to chip away at. I replied, 'That may well be your opinion but it's not mine. I believe Tom Crean was an integral part of their expeditions. And if it weren't for men like Tom, who were prepared to go and push the envelope and expand our human knowledge of where we live and how we live, the likes of you would still be living in a mud hut.' Later, my cousin from Dublin came up to me and said, 'Aidan, you gave your soul out there today and then you get a bollix like that who doesn't appreciate what you've done. Why not cut out the question-and-answer sessions afterwards?' I thought long and hard about it. This man had dragged his animosity, his blinkered perspective into my show because I had invited his comments. It had hurt me quite a lot and I didn't want to open myself up to more of the same. I decided to take my cousin's suggestion and omit the question-and-answer sessions as a regular post-show event.

I did not let this nanosecond of negativity spoil my delight overall. I felt that both Galway shows had gone well, with my adrenaline bringing out more of the humour. During each performance the audience was very responsive and afterwards they made some appreciative comments and told me how they had really connected with the show. My mother was over the moon about the whole thing. Back at the house, she was buttering some soda bread when she said to me, 'I suppose you were right to give up the bank.' It was a wonderful thing to hear. After their earlier worries about me changing careers, my parents could at last see that I had not been wasting my time. Over the years that I have now been performing Tom Crean, they have been hugely supportive of me and the show. From the beginning, my father was very taken with Tom. Along with my mother, he saw the show countless times and could probably have told the stories himself. It's never quite the same on any night and I sometimes vary which anecdotes I tell, but if my father was in the audience he would tell me off roundly if I missed out any of his favourite bits.

My mother became an integral part of keeping Tom on the road. Every time I returned to Ireland on tour, she would mend my worn-out costume. Today, I still wear the same mitts, the same trousers, all the same clothes as I started in. I'm quite superstitious about it. My mother has patiently sewn and patched all these sweat-ravaged garments. It's not easy to patch moleskin, but Mammy would somehow manage to shore up the bottom area on my trousers, sometimes with patches that weren't the right colour. But then, Tom and the men would have mended their own trousers so, I reasoned, any imperfections would just add a realistic roughness to the whole thing. The only thing that escaped the darning needle is my jumper, which has now lost its shape entirely and is full of holes. There's something very poignant to me about that gaping, shapeless jumper. On the subject of jumpers, I thought for many years that Scott and his officers were wearing 'polar-necked' jumpers. As Tom, I used to say, 'We went up to London and the officers demanded their polar-necked jumpers.' It wasn't a play on words, I thought it was a happy coincidence. I was quite disappointed when I discovered my mistake. Polo-necked? Really?

If Galway had been a little triumph, I was only too aware that the audiences were a tad biased. As I drove to my next venue in Listowel, I was interested to see what strangers, a 'real' audience if you like, would make of the show. In my pocket I had a cheque from the Taibhdhearc theatre for €1,200, the amount owed to me from the sale of tickets once the theatre rent was paid. I couldn't believe it: €1,200 for two nights' work! It felt like a fortune to me. It would have taken me weeks to earn that amount of money from my museum shifts. I remember thinking, 'I wouldn't mind a bit more of that!'

The theatre in Listowel is in a lovely old Protestant church in the middle of town. Since it is in Tom's home county of Kerry, the play had generated some interest and sixty people had booked. Not bad for an unknown play. Most significantly, they were not my family and friends. Geraint, my boss from the museums, had flown over to see the show and I was keen that he should like it. I think this was the first time any of Geraint's museum work had gone into a commercial place and his opinion was important to me. The show went well and afterwards Geraint and I tried in vain to find a restaurant in Listowel that was open. We ended up buying takeaway pizza and taking it back to one of our hotel rooms. We talked a lot about the show. Geraint had loved it and we talked about how I should pick up the pace in the second half and drive the story on. Geraint also wondered if I should make the piece more theatrical but I was of the opinion (and still am) that Tom's magnificent tale doesn't need embellishment: the simple storytelling style seems to be the most powerful way of getting it across.

The fourth and last venue on my mini tour was the South Pole Inn where I would once again do the show in the room above the pub. It was good to return to Annascaul and meet up again with Eileen Percival, the pub landlady, who has dedicated her tenure there to Tom's memory. I showed Geraint all the places associated with Tom: the Black Lake, the mountains, his burial place. Performing in Tom's former home, to fifty or so people, was no less extraordinary than the previous time. If anything, it was possibly better as it was not totally wrapped up in nervous energy and was a more substantial piece of theatre with a better structure to it.

I was proud of my first tour of the show and especially glad that my family and friends had seen it. It vindicated my decision to leave a pensionable job to pursue what others probably perceived as some mad dream in England. Friends in Galway told me how they had not understood what I had been doing in England, or what the museum work was all about. But now that they had seen the show, they said they totally got it. I had also been very encouraged by the reaction in Listowel and Annascaul, where audiences who had no connection with me or my family had really seemed to engage with it. It gave me a reasonable amount of confidence that a modern Irish audience might actually want to listen to this story of daring Edwardian explorers. And, as the icing on the cake, I had earned a total of around €2,000 for my efforts

– the equivalent of six weeks' museum wages from five performances.

But before I could feel too pleased with myself, I had an unfortunate brush with the Irish law. It was 9 a.m. and I was driving from Annascaul to get the ferry back to England when I was flagged down by a Garda. Unluckily for me, Ireland had just introduced speeding points and I had apparently been going too fast. Just 70 mph on a dual carriageway, Officer. He told me I had to pay a fine and wrote it on my licence. I was staying that night just outside Dublin with my old school friend Mike Higgins and I asked him if he would go to the garda station the next day and pay the fine for me. I was fearful that I would be coming off the ferry at some point in the future and would be collared by the police because I owed them thousands of euro in late fees. My own brother Raymond was a garda at the time and when I told him some months later how worried I'd been, he laughed his head off. He said there was probably a woman somewhere, say Tipperary, who deals with all the unpaid fines. What do you think she is going to do, asks my brother, when she sees an English number plate and English address with an Irish name? Use all of her considerable admin powers to hunt me down like a criminal, I venture? No, she would tear it up of course, laughs my brother. I am, it seems, a law-abiding adventurer.

5
TOM THE BRAVE

He was dead. And I remember going and scooping up his little body in my arms and thinking, 'This is someone's son, someone's brother, and this forsaken place has taken him from them.' And I couldn't help it, they came again, flooding out of my eyes all together, red-hot scalding tears that splashed and bounced onto his chest and splashed onto his face and beard and it must have been the heat of those tears 'cos didn't one of his eyes open and he looked up at me and said 'Crean, you're a soft git.' He wasn't dead at all but he was that close, that close.

From *Tom Crean – Antarctic Explorer* (Aidan Dooley)

The Antarctic snow was warmed by the tears of Tom Crean on more than one occasion. Unafraid of showing his feelings, or perhaps simply unable to hide them, Crean must have cut an extraordinary figure among those stoical English Edwardians. Fond of children and animals, quick to cry and unfailingly cheery, Tom had a softness that sat quite happily with his rock-solid strength. He was a pragmatist when necessary, shooting his beloved puppies rather than letting them starve to death on the ice, but he may well have shed some tears at the same time. The Antarctic would give a man every good reason to cry. Even the reserved Captain Scott understood Crean's salty outburst of emotion when, within striking distance of the main prize, Scott finally told Tom that he wasn't going to be the first Irishman to set foot on the South Pole but must head back to base camp with Evans and Lashly. And again, who could have blamed Tom for shedding tears at the pitiful discovery, ten months later, of the small green tent enclosing the frost-ravaged bodies of Scott, Wilson and Bowers in their final resting place.

The tears he cried over the apparent death of Lieutenant Teddy Evans on their harrowing trek back from the polar plateau with Bill Lashly were happily premature, but they no doubt helped to fuel what I believe to be Tom's finest, most heroic, hour on the ice. Tom, Evans and Lashly had nearly made it to the South Pole, were indeed only 150 miles away, when they learned they were not to be in Scott's final party. It is hard to imagine what the desolate trio might have been thinking on 4 January 1912 when, after sending their five colleagues on their way south with three huge cheers, they turned around and began their grim 750-mile trek back to base.

Hope can steel you against many a hardship. But now, with all ambitions of polar glory gone, it was a return trip tinged with despair and the punishing sub-zero conditions must have bitten very cruelly. Any feelings of disappointment were quickly overshadowed, however, by their ensuing battle to survive. It was, in so many ways, an unfair battle for Crean, Lashly and Evans. The dispirited three were a man and a sledge meter down, having lost both to Scott's party. With three men instead of four and only one navigator, the party was extremely vulnerable. To make matters worse, they had already been out on the ice, dragging sledges, for a gruelling two months, so they had no reserves of energy for the task ahead. Food would not be stoking their engines, as the rations were woefully inadequate. They were probably consuming around

The *James Caird*. It was loaned by Dulwich College in London (where Ernest Shackleton went to school) to the National Maritime Museum in Greenwich. Aidan performed right beside it when he first started playing Tom Crean, in 2000/2001.

3,000 calories if they were lucky, less than half of what they needed, given where they were and what they were doing. The lacerating polar winter was fast approaching, biting at their heels, so time was of the essence.

Dragging their 400lb sledge-load in a fragile silence, the men withstood plummeting temperatures, snow-blindness, hunger and bone-weary exhaustion. They even outwitted death by sledging down a 2,000ft icefall and emerging with all limbs intact. With courage, luck and a single-minded will to live, the trio kept going against all the odds. But they hadn't reckoned on scurvy. In theory, it should have been Tom Crean who got the dreaded disease because he was being depleted of more vitamins, being bigger than the other two but on the same rations. I remember once having a chat with an audience member after a show and I was saying how incredible it was that Tom did not succumb to scurvy. Was that luck? Or something in his constitution that protected him? The man I was talking to explained that they couldn't afford tea in the west of Ireland when Tom was growing up, so they drank nothing but water and milk and had a diet of mainly fish. Maybe that was the secret of Tom's extraordinary ability to survive. It was, in fact, Lieutenant Evans who was stricken by scurvy and by mid February he was perilously ill and unable to walk. Disobeying Evans' command to leave him and save themselves, Crean and Lashly laid the officer on the sledge and, with a superhuman effort, managed to drag Evans and themselves to within 40 miles of Hut Point. They could not have done any more for their dying comrade, but still it wasn't enough. With four or five days of man-hauling still to do and barely any food, their fate looked bleak. And, it was at this point, after some 1,500 miles on the ice, with all energy spent, that Tom Crean showed his true mettle. He would try and finish the journey alone.

The stakes could not have been higher, nor his chance of success any lower, as he set off for Hut Point, leaving Lashly to look after Evans. The malnourished man had just three biscuits and two sticks of chocolate by way of food. He had no tent because sleep was a luxury he could not afford. He had no compass: the mountains would be his guide along with, hopefully, the marker posts laid by the expedition team on the way out. His courage goes beyond words, but Crean also had, like Shackleton, an instinct for survival that meant he kept his head under pressure. Explorers have told me that being exposed to severe cold can affect your brain and have a disorientating effect, a bit like underwater divers exposed to nitrogen. It makes you wonder if Scott might have made some different decisions away from the ice. Tom, however, was still able to think clearly, as he demonstrated on this lonely journey to Hut Point. Having made good progress, there came a moment when he could clearly see his goal, let's say the hut lay some 2 miles in the distance. But between Tom and safety lay a white mass of ice – sea ice – which Tom knew he could not trust to hold his weight because some of it was still slushy from the summer. Heartbreaking though it was, he shunned the most direct route over the sea ice and instead made his weary way up Observation Hill. This route may have taken him three times as long but it was far less risky and Tom's decision could well have saved his life.

And at last, after nineteen tortuous hours, Tom stumbled into Hut Point and safety. Within half an hour of his arrival, a ferocious blizzard began raging outside, a storm that would have undoubtedly tolled Tom's death knell had he been caught in it. The storm raged until a day and half later when, on 20 February 1912, a dog team (minus Tom, who was in no fit state to go out, despite volunteering to do so) was at last sent to find Evans and Lashly who had hung onto life in their tiny tent. Both Crean and Lashly were to receive an Albert Medal for saving the life of Lieutenant Evans, but it was Crean's stupendous solo trek that had saved all three of them. With typical understatement, Tom told his friend in a letter that his 'long legs did the trick'.

I am totally in awe of Tom's courage. After all those months on the ice and physically on his last legs, who knows how he summoned the strength to make that journey and think his way out of danger. Out on the ice, negative thoughts could kill you. It's not that you need to put any fears or doubts to one side, you just can't have them in the first place. Staying positive is essential and Tom seemed to have an innate ability to do so. His stoical good cheer must have been uplifting to his comrades, even if his singing ability left a lot to be desired. According to colleagues' diaries, Tom had a habit of singing, out of tune, in even the direst situations. If you were aboard a small, leaking boat that was being tossed about on the ferocious Southern Ocean, I would imagine that Tom's tuneless renditions would either be a comfort, or so irritating that you might be tempted to push him overboard. You would, however, always want the Irish giant on board when the going got tough.

In 2014 two British men, explorer Ben Saunders and former rugby player Tarka L'Herpiniere, became the first people in history to retrace the ill-fated steps of Captain Scott and his men. Walking 1,795 miles to the South Pole and back, the pair set the record for the longest polar journey on foot. Their achievement was extraordinary but it also served to highlight just how incredible the achievements of those Edwardian explorers were. Saunders and L'Herpiniere had state-of-the-art, waterproof clothes and tents, not to mention constant contact with the outside world via laptops specially adapted for daily blogging. Unlike Crean and company, the 21st-century explorers were well nourished, but they still lost weight despite consuming 6,000 calories per day. And they also had fresh supplies flown in during their return journey when their food stock became low. Dangerous and punishing as their trek was, Saunders and L'Herpiniere knew they were not totally without support and, if the worst happened, they could be removed to safety. Says Saunders: 'You can only have a sense of awe at Scott and his men. They didn't have any communications; they had no chance of being rescued. They might as well have been on Pluto as at the South Pole.' If ever I am in danger of becoming too delighted with myself and the show, I only need think about Tom's mighty achievements to be put firmly in my place.

6
MY JOURNEY SOUTH

And the English, ah they are not as bad as we Irish make them out to be. I am not saying we don't have to keep an eye on a couple of them, don't get me wrong! But on the whole … 'cos no sooner were we back in London town, the King of England himself beckoned Bill and myself to Buckingham Palace and put a medal on my chest. A medal which, as he pinned, he said to me under his breath, 'This is my father's medal, we give it to our heroes.' And that's what they read out in the citation in front of the King and all … 'These two men are heroes as they refused to obey the officer and abandon him.' Tom Crean Albert Medal – and they still don't have a clue who the hell I am!

From *Tom Crean – Antarctic Explorer* (Aidan Dooley)

Even if Tom didn't trumpet his own remarkable achievements, I found it unbelievable that we were not doing so on his behalf a century later. All he merited in South, the Maritime Museum's 2001 major polar exhibition, was one reference. A single mention! But perhaps I should be thankful for that, because without my anger at the injustice of it, I might never have written my show. And without my work in museums, I might never have even thought about Tom Crean. It certainly had not been on my list of dream acting jobs when I left drama school: dress up as a historical character and talk to visitors at the Science Museum. In fact, the idea of working as an actor in any museum had never entered my mind. I suppose I left drama school in the late 1980s full of naive hope and ambitions, much the same as any new graduate. It didn't take long for the profession's harsh realities to reveal themselves. I felt that I had learned a lot at Guildford – I had even won an award for 'Best Actor in the Year' – and I left drama school with the belief that, yes, I did deserve to be a professional actor.

This new-found confidence was knocked out of me cruelly when I applied for a job at the Dundee Rep Theatre. They were doing John Millington Synge's classic *The Playboy of the Western World*, and I was up for the lead part of Christy Mahon.

Guildford
School of
Acting and Dance

Aidan Dooley

has successfully completed the
one-year postgraduate course
and has been awarded
the Diploma of the
Guildford School of Acting
and Dance

Winner of Postgraduate Acting Prize.

PRINCIPAL *Miriam Grawnt   July 1988*

FOUNDER *Bice Bellairs* HEAD OF COURSE *Cathy Ingram*

PRESENTED BY

Aidan's acting diploma from the Guilford School of Acting and Dance.

That role and Hamlet were the parts that I really hankered to play. It was a great audition. I came away thinking I had it, that the job was surely mine. A few days went by, then a week, then two weeks and I had heard nothing. I will never forget the pain of it. When I phoned up the theatre and spoke to a secretary or assistant, she said casually, 'Oh, if you've not received a contract by now you haven't got it.' I don't know what was worse, not getting the part, or the insensitive way I was given the news, as if it wasn't in the least bit important. The experience really knocked me, took the wind completely out of my sails and stopped me from applying for jobs for a long time because I couldn't bear the thought of going through that searing disappointment again. I clearly needed to develop a thicker skin.

My first job was a bit mad and definitely less creatively fulfilling than I might have wished. It was close to Christmas 1988 and involved touring around in a van and taking a pantomime to working men's clubs as part of their Christmas entertainment for families. I was paid the princely sum of £110 a week to perform three shows a day six days a week to kids enjoying a sweet-induced sugar rush. Every morning, I would be picked up in the van outside Golders Green tube station and driven by one of the other actors to the venue. Amid

Aidan's first 'head shot', taken in 1988 when he was twenty-five.

screaming children who were off their heads on E-numbers, we actors would be setting up for the show, which was enhanced by a solitary floodlight and two static microphones into which we would try and deliver all our lines. I both loved and hated it. We were not being treated particularly well by the company we worked for and it was a slog, but on the other hand, it wasn't the bank. I still carried the recent memory of working 9 to 5 and at least this was an adventure of sorts.

I know a lot of people think it's a glamorous thing to be an actor, that you are lucky to have found your passion and so on. But honestly, having no money, no security and very little control over your career is not so very glamorous and can be brutally unkind. I'm not complaining: it's a sacrifice we willingly make and when you are having a good night out on that stage it's a feeling like no other. Looking back, though, when we first left drama school, it was pretty tough to make ends meet and things were touch and go for a while. We sometimes had no idea where next month's rent was coming from. As well as the difficulty of finding acting work, there's the problem of finding a job you can do in between. Miriam and I, who were engaged by this time and deeply in love, had to try and find employment where no one relied on us, just in case

Aidan on stage in the Assembly Rooms at the Edinburgh Fringe Festival, August 2006.

' "Sir, how far have we dragged and how long have we been dragging?" And Shackleton shouted back, "We've dragged for sixteen hours and we have travelled one mile" ... One mile. Four hundred would kill us all together ... Fortunately he put that plan to bed.'

TOP: A ticket for the play's first run in the Olympia Theatre, Dublin, January 2007. Aidan has appeared there six times to date. BELOW: The advert that appeared regularly in *The Irish Times* in 2007 helped promote the show nationwide.

RIGHT: Actor and presenter Tony Robinson presents Aidan Dooley with the coveted Fringe First award at the Edinburgh Fringe Festival, August 2006. *THE SCOTSMAN*

BELOW: The Tom Crean set at the Civic Theatre in Tallaght, 2004. As Aidan toured, the lighting evolved with help from Pierce Kavanagh at Andrews Lane Theatre but this was when the moon was first seen, following the suggestion of the Civic's techie, Mick Doyle.

TOP: Aidan in the dressing room at the Everyman Theatre in Cork in 2011, waiting to be called to the stage.

BELOW: There are 1,200 seats in the Olympia Theatre in Dublin. It is humbling, daunting and exciting to stand and stare out at this magnificent Victorian auditorium.

LEFT: The *Fram* in Oslo. This is the ship on which Roald Amundsen sailed south in his successful bid to reach the South Pole in December 1911. Aidan performed extracts on the *Fram* as part of the 2015 St Patrick's Day celebrations, courtesy of the Irish Embassy in Norway.

BELOW: December 2010, on the windswept mountain pass between Fortuna Bay and Stromness on South Georgia, just before the whaling station can be seen. Aidan wore modern thermals beneath his Burberry.

TOP: Aidan stands at the grave of Sir Ernest Shackleton in Grytviken, South Georgia in 2010.

BELOW: Still in costume, on a tiny rocky beach on Elephant Island, near to where twenty-two of the *Endurance* crew waited four and a half months before being rescued.

TOP: Aidan performs beside the newly unveiled statue of Tom Crean as part of the Midwinter Dinner celebrations in Annascaul, December 2003.

RIGHT: On stage in Siamsa Tíre, Tralee, in October 2001, for the show's first theatre performance.

'You will sweat and the moment you stop dragging or digging or building, that sweat will turn to ice, and that ice can be right against your skin and that can kill you.'

On stage in Siamsa Tíre, Tralee, in October 2001.
'"Well, surely, surely," I say, "you must have heard of Tom Crean?" Arrah … They look at me like I've got four heads. But 'tis my own fault, I never kept a diary.'

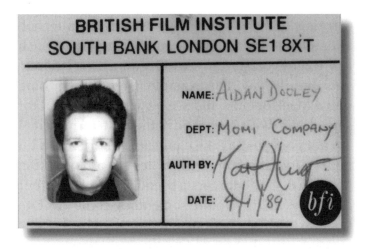

BRITISH FILM INSTITUTE
SOUTH BANK LONDON SE1 8XT

NAME: AIDAN DOOLEY

DEPT: MOMI COMPANY

AUTH BY: MatHumer

DATE: 4/1/89

bfi

Aidan's ID for London's Museum of the Moving Image.

an acting role came up and we had to leave them in the lurch. We both worked for a catering company, Miriam as a waitress and I was sometimes given the job of porter. I will never forget working one night for a woman in Golders Green. She had her family coming over for Passover and she had hired staff for what was essentially a family meal. She had notions. Her family were obviously embarrassed to be greeted at their mother's house by Miriam, who was standing to attention, in uniform, in the hallway. But we were both paid the princely sum of £50 so it was worth the embarrassment.

As the kitchen porter I was paid £2.50 an hour. It was a tough job – endless pot washing and carrying catering loads to and from job after job after job all over London – and when you get such low wages you start to see everything in relation to your hourly pay. For example, I remember going into a MacDonald's and seeing a Big Mac Meal for something like £2.99. And I thought to myself, I am not going to pay the equivalent of one and a bit hours of washing crap off plates for a bloody Big Mac Meal. John Morgan, a friend from my amateur days in Dublin, would sometimes come over to London and take us out for dinner, which was a massive treat that made us deliriously happy.

They were testing times, struggling to make ends meet and keep our heads above water. But life was still good, I wasn't at the bank, I was madly in love with this wonderful woman Miriam and we were planning to get married. Just after the panto tour, I found another job that helped pay for our wedding. I started working at MOMI, the Museum of the Moving Image near Waterloo Bridge in London, which was centred around the history of technology and media including cinema. It doesn't exist any more, but at that time it had just started using actors as part of the visitor experience. We played different historical characters and would interact with people as they went into different rooms. I played a Russian soldier on a train and I chatted to people about Russian cinema, which would be playing on a loop.

At MOMI we would be out on the floor for three hours at a stretch. In many ways we were glorified museum attendants, though the manager encouraged us to talk to people as much as possible. We didn't have much in the way of scripts. However, I had done my homework on Russian cinema so could talk about that a bit, but I soon learned that I would become very bored very quickly unless I really threw myself into the work. While some actors remained fairly uninvolved for their three hours, I became this positive, bubbly character who chatted away animatedly to everyone who came my way. It was self-preservation, really; if I hadn't completely gone for it at MOMI, constantly finding new things to say, new ways to engage people and make them laugh, I would have been insanely bored. I was entertaining myself as well as the public. You become a sort of performing clown that you can just switch on and off, which is a useful skill. You have your gags and your patter and you just turn a switch as soon as you walk into the space. Not all museum visitors wanted to engage with this character. I soon developed an instinct for those who just wanted to be left alone to look at the museum exhibits and artefacts. I discovered that I enjoyed this kind of improvising, that I could think on my feet and always come up with something to say. Working at MOMI gave me particular skills and experience that would prove very useful. This was where the very kernel of my Tom Crean play was conceived – in the storytelling skills, the direct address to the audience, the sense of being spontaneously in the moment, of using elements of my own personality – all of which would become integral to my show.

I left MOMI after two lengthy contracts and it was then that reality began to bite. My new wife and I tried for a while to live in Manchester and when that didn't work out, owing to lack of work up north, we found ourselves back in London, penniless and sleeping in a friend's spare room, Miriam in the single bed and me on the floor. This was no start to married life and eventually we managed to get our own place, a tiny, freezing flat we rented in Edmonton, north London. It was a dump but it was ours and we made it homely. Finding money was a constant struggle and I eventually took some temping work at the Bank of Ireland because I was so fed up of being skint. Every day I made the journey from Edmonton to Croydon. The bank manager there seemed to like me. He would bring me up for drinks on a Friday afternoon and chat to me about my plans. Looking back, I think he would

Aidan and Miriam Cooper on their wedding day, 23 September 1989.

have offered me a full-time job had he not seen how pointless this was. But at the time, I did not notice his subtle hints and suggestions, because I was so focused on being an actor and trying to find acting work. The fact was, no matter how bad things were, I was never tempted to go back to the 9 to 5 at the bank; this was a temp job that was simply keeping the wolf from the door. I was grateful for it but wasn't ever going back to it fully.

Eventually I heard from a friend that the Science Museum in London's South Kensington was looking for actors for a similar type of interactive work as I had done at MOMI. So I wrote a letter (yes, an actual letter, remember those?) to the man running it, a Welshman called Geraint Thomas. Much later he told me that among all the many letters he received mine stood out because I signed off with the words 'God Bless'. I have no idea why I did that. It wasn't even my usual sign-off, but it just seemed much warmer than the usual. Anyway, it did the trick and so I began to immerse myself in the world of 'live interpretation' at the museums. One of the characters I played was Victorian plumber Thomas Crapper. We had a little script to learn but, as I discovered at MOMI, it was much more interesting to go off script and improvise. I was always trying to come up with stories that would hold people's

Miriam and Aidan in 1996 in Stockholm, where they visited as part of an educational theatre trip.

attention, these half-mad, half-wonderful notions that I would work and hone to perfection. I think one of the reasons museum work was so enjoyable was because I enjoy people, especially making people smile. As Thomas Crapper, I had all this banter and would show people my lovely laminated sanitary-ware catalogue from 1903. I talked about the different toilet pans with relish. 'All you need to do is sit on it and relax,' I would gush. 'Just look at the beauty of it.' Well, it entertained me. Another character I played, in the London Transport Museum in Covent Garden, was an Irish tunnel miner called J. J. who taught people about how the underground and tube systems were built in London. I loved playing him because I made him funny and wrote many a gag for him. Though the character was fictional, he was based on a study I'd read of real-life Irish immigrants from around 1906. The study included some of their letters home, which were a vivid and invaluable insight into the conditions and the rough times they experienced as they tried to make a living in London in the early 1900s. My J. J. was from Sligo and a real joker. I would talk to the gathered public as if they were trainee tunnel miners and let them know what they've got coming to them when they start work in the mornin'!

Working as an actor in the museums was like a cross between street theatre and stand-up. You were often performing in a public space, so you had to grab people's attention as they were passing by and try to hold on to it. It was a great lesson in how to captivate an audience. As demand for this kind of museum work grew during the early 1990s we started to write short plays and perform them. The challenge of writing these scripts was how to make

Aidan in the Science Museum in London, in the guise of Victorian plumber Thomas Crapper in the early 1990s.

the most unlikely subject, such as the manufacture of steel, interesting and entertaining. I discovered that I had an ability born out of an innate curiosity to find the joy and fun in even the most mundane of briefs. So *that's* how concrete's formed, wow, I never knew that … It was work that did not suit everyone and some actors just could not get on with it. For those who worked regularly at the museums, there was always a sense that it was a great stopgap between more conventional acting jobs.

The museums became my bread-and-butter work, but I would still go off and do a theatre job if it came up. I soon realised that my agent was pigeonholing me by only putting me up for Irish roles, which at the time limited my options considerably. But I did land some good and enjoyable theatre jobs. I had a lovely time working for Show of Strength, a fringe company in Bristol with whom I did a couple of plays. I made it to the bright lights of the West End in Brian Friel's brilliant play *Philadelphia, Here I Come!*, which first came to the London stage at the King's Head Theatre in Islington and eventually transferred to Wyndham's Theatre for a sell-out run. I played a character called Tom – that name follows me …

The cast was a really talented group of actors, many going on to long and successful theatre careers. George Heslin runs Origin Theatre in New York, Rouri Conaghan is a National Theatre actor amongst many other roles, Dave Duffy has been a regular on RTÉ's *Fair City* for many years, while Jonathan Arun is a successful theatre agent. It was obvious even then that Brendan Coyle was en route to a glittering acting career. Enigmatic and very talented, Brendan could hold an audience in the palm of his hand. Orla Brady was similarly gifted and poised for success. Always having a laugh, we

West End, here I come! A flyer for Aidan's West End debut in 1992.

PHILADELPHIA
Here I Come!

by

BRIAN FRIEL

Madge	**PAULINE DELANY**
Gareth O'Donnell { in Public	**JONATHAN ARUN**
in Private	**BRENDAN COYLE**
S.B. O'Donnell	**EAMON KELLY**
Kate Doogan	**ORLA BRADY**
Senator Doogan	**DENIS QUILLIGAN**
Master Boyle	**PATRICK DUGGAN**
Lizzy Sweeney	**VALERIE HERMANNI**
Con Sweeney	**DAVID DUFFY**
Ben Burton	**EDGAR DAVIES**
Ned	**RUAIRI CONAGHAN**
Tom	**AIDAN DOOLEY**
Joe	**GEORGE HESLIN**
Canon Mick O'Byrne	**FRANK DUNNE**
Directed by	**DAN CRAWFORD**
Designed by	**NIGEL HOOK**
Costumes designed by	**MARGUERITE SMITH**
Lighting by	**LEONARD TUCKER**
Movement by	**DAVID TOGURI**
Assistant Director and Casting	**DONAL O'MATHUNA**
Company Stage Manager	**KEVIN GRANT**
Deputy Stage Manager	**SALLY HARDY**
Assistant Stage Managers and Understudies	**CLAIRE FISHER**
	JAMES MOLLOY
Understudy	**MAURA O'SULLIVAN**
Wardrobe	**KRISTI WARWICK**
Production Carpenters	**DAVID HOLLAND**
	ROBIN JEFFREY
Production Electrician	**JASON TAYLOR**

The action takes place in a small village in Ireland

The play will run for 2 hours and 20 minutes
with two intervals – one of 15 minutes and one of 7 minutes

The cast list from the programme for *Philadelphia, Here I Come!*
in Wyndham's Theatre, summer 1992.

would all hang out in the green room and, after the show, the pub. We were together for many months in what felt like a big family and we are all still in contact to this day.

From the moment we started rehearsing it, we knew *Philadelphia* was something special and we all understood it and knew how our contribution to the play would work. It was a huge success, giving me a taste of West End theatrical glamour and it would have been easy to think we'd hit the big time. One of the other young actors was incredulous that I was keeping up my museum work during the day and performing in the West End at night. 'What are you still doing that for, we're on the up,' he said. But once *Philadelphia* had finished, we slid down that slippery pole of success. I had a great credit on my CV but I was once again a jobbing actor looking for work. So there was no way I was giving up the museums, my 'keeping the fridge full' work.

Sometimes my heart would sink when I got a theatre role because getting time off from the museums was always difficult. The boss, Geraint, would never make it easy for you, always giving a heavy sigh when you told him you needed some time off. You had to find another actor to fill your slots and then when you came back from whatever it was you had been doing, there was always the worry that he wouldn't use you any more, and you would have to work your way back onto the museum rota. So, as much as I wanted to do other acting jobs, I would apply for them half hoping that I wouldn't get them so that I wouldn't have to go through the rigmarole of disappointing Geraint.

All this while, Miriam was working with a schools Shakespeare touring company and doing museum work as well. When our bundle of joy – Liam – came along I decided to work full-time in the museums. It was not that my aspirations as a more conventional actor had vanished – I still would have dearly loved to play Christy Mahon or Hamlet – but now I had a family to feed and perhaps that Dooley pragmatism kicked in. When I left the bank I had thought to myself, if I can make a living out of any aspect of performing then I will have succeeded. And I was making a fair and reliable living as museum characters. Deciding to do it full-time, however, was a significant step because it meant sacrificing my acting aspirations. When I was scratching around washing dishes as a porter, there was still hope that the call would come from *EastEnders*, but if you take yourself out of the game altogether you know it's never, ever, going to happen. Many actors will tell you that one of the biggest headaches is not so much trying to land the job, hard though that is, but the decision to accept it once it is offered. Often, this will involve you taking time off from your temporary or freelance job, which never goes down well. Since many of us have to do other work to survive, you constantly run the risk of biting the hand that feeds you and letting people down so you can go off and act. You constantly have to weigh up whether the role is worth losing the goodwill of the people you're currently working for.

This all fed into my decision to take myself out of mainstream acting for the foreseeable future. As well as a regular, reliable income, full-time museum acting work would give me peace of mind. It was a decision that, as a father, I was very happy to make. So there I was, a dedicated 'live interpreter', happily doing my days as Thomas Crapper and other historical characters in various London museums. Miriam was doing the same work and our joint wages enabled us (just) to buy a house in Rochester, Kent. We formed our own theatre company called Play On Words with Tony and Lynn Brown (lifelong friends), touring Shakespeare workshops to schools all over the country and drama classes for youth groups. Our hope was to introduce his plays to students as a positive and fun experience. We have a ninety-minute 'Introduction to Shakespeare' that starts with the gore of *Macbeth*, then the tragedy of *Romeo and Juliet*, followed by the slapstick fun of *A Midsummer Night's Dream* and finally the politics of *Julius Caesar*. We always perform a good scene from each play and tell the story outline in an entertaining, almost pantomimic way. It goes down a treat and I always will remember a young lad in a tough school in Sheppey, Kent, coming up to us afterwards and asking, 'So where do I get these stories then?' – result! Our youth theatre and summer school work has been a constant with us for years. Running schools in Guernsey since 1990, it was our family summer holiday for two decades. Miriam and I love bringing the joy of performance to young people, seeing it build their confidence, their self-belief and helping them to be a better, more fulfilled person as they progress to adulthood. I never managed to get *Hamlet* into our repertoire but hey, I use the last line of the play to sign off every tour of Tom Crean. At the end of every run, I send a text to Miriam saying, 'The rest is silence.'

I was also part of the creative team in the ill-fated Millennium Experience in the Greenwich Dome in 2000. It was the same sort of interactive theatre work that I did at the museums and we performed small theatre pieces around the Dome at appointed times. I remember vividly one of my characters,

Aidan's newly arrived daughter Nancy with her dad and big brother Liam at the first Tom Crean performance day in the National Maritime Museum, Greenwich, in 2001.

a mad blood-splattered surgeon trying to piece together a skeleton companion called Sir Hinge, in order to enlighten people about our organs and their functions. Alas, we lasted only three months of the twelve that had been promised because the Dome never lived up to the hype that had been created around it. It got off to a disastrous start as people queued for hours only to find that the whole experience was not nearly as much fun as it should have been. As a result, they had to slash costs and contracts along with it. With little foreseeable income, we nevertheless had another child, our wonderful daughter Nancy, which made me even more sure that I had made the right decision to put aside my acting ambitions. There may have still been a tiny flame, a dream of playing Hamlet, burning away quietly inside me, but for those few years I was happy enough with the life I had chosen. Then along came Tom Crean, who was about to make my life richer in so many ways.

When I first started creating Tom for the Maritime Museum back in 2001, he really was a mystery because so little had been written about him. Unlike some of his fellow explorers, he had not kept a diary and he seemed to be a man of few words. He let his actions do the talking. And even though, over time, I have gleaned more insights from people with close connections to him, Tom the man remains something of an enigma. There are many things we will never know about him. Behind his respectful silence about his two bosses, what did he really think of Scott and Shackleton, for example? Why did he keep getting promoted and then demoted in his early navy years? What was his lowest point on the ice?

The show is not a factual biography of Tom: it is a piece of storytelling theatre based around him. Similarly, I am not doing an impersonation of him, not least because we actually know so little about him. The Tom I play in the show is a blend of fact, supposition and my own personality, though we are different in so many ways. It is quite ironic that I am playing someone so physically intrepid, because I am most definitely not. I have bad knees, having had cartilage removed in my twenties following a footballing injury, and don't even really like going for long walks. I take Jigsaw, our springer spaniel, out every day purely because she has to be walked. We always go to the same place and while sometimes we might do two loops of the meadow, that's the only variation. You won't find me roaming off the beaten track very often just for the sake of it. I like mountains, by which I mean I like looking at them and I would love to see the view from them if someone would transport me up there. Even then, I might be in trouble because I have no head for heights. I remember one of my first dates with Miriam when we were drama students and I tried to impress her by showing her the sights from the top of St Paul's Cathedral. We had to climb up wrought-iron steps that had far too much fresh air between them for my poor pumping heart. Eventually, the penny dropped for Miriam that I wasn't admiring the spectacular view of London at all, but was instead pinned, sweating, to the wall. Needless to say, I don't venture up many high places, whether made by man or nature.

I think Tom and I probably have very different energy, too. You get the impression that Tom could have probably sat very happily in companionable silence for an hour or so, whereas I could never do that; I would always be tempted to fill in the gaps in any conversation out of insecurity or embarrassment. Nor do I share Tom's cheery optimism. I was once given the nickname Happy by a cast member in a play I was doing a few years ago. My fellow actor was being ironic, of course, and was referring to the fact that I was never completely satisfied with the performance we'd just done. After every show I would be picking it apart, saying things like, 'That scene didn't work so well tonight', or 'What were we doing there?'

As an actor, I always think I could do better, which is probably true because no performance is perfect. Having been on the road with Tom for over a decade now, however, I think I have learned to be kinder to myself and forgive myself the odd imperfection or two. Even so, I didn't really allow myself to revel in the audience's enthusiastic appreciation of the show. In the early days, especially, when there were overwhelming reactions, I felt that I needed to keep my feet on the ground. I am really happy that people like it so much that they would give me standing ovations, but I suppose I never wanted to become big-headed and lose the humility I feel I need for my performance. I would sometimes say in post-show chats, 'I am not fit to tie the laces of Tom Crean, but then again if he was here now he wouldn't talk to you for two hours as I have just done.' Ultimately, no matter what my involvement in its creation, I know that the show has been a hit because of the story itself and that story belongs to Tom Crean, not me.

7
A BITE OF THE BIG APPLE

And there are those, when I come home, who say, 'Why do you do it, Tom? Why would you go to the last place on earth? Is there summat wrong with you?' And I say, 'You've never been … but you've just said why, haven't you: the last place on earth. Can you not imagine,' I say to them, 'merely imagine standing, standing where no one had ever stood before, to see a vista never before seen, wouldn't that be magnificent? To be the first Irishman …' And I got that close, that close, that close on a map. One hundred and forty-five nautical miles.

From *Tom Crean – Antarctic Explorer* (Aidan Dooley)

The receptionist at a Cork arts centre was just as inhospitable as the Antarctic terrain. 'Ah no, I don't imagine we would be interested in that,' she sighed, a forbidding blend of bored disinterest and prickly ferocity. I was not having much luck trying to take Tom on the road. After returning home from my little 2002 tour to Athy, Galway and Listowel, I was all fired up to do another, bigger tour of my show. Unlike Tom, I was not setting my sights on distant horizons but was trying to book venues close to home, in Ireland. I started to phone around various theatres, including the Cork arts centre with the frosty receptionist. But sure, you couldn't really blame her for not wanting to take an unknown show with an unknown actor, even if he was proud of the fact that his mam had packed out a Galway theatre for a couple of nights. My approach had been a bit half-baked and none too convincing, something along the lines of, 'Er, I'm doing this play about an Antarctic fella, would you be interested …? No, you wouldn't be interested? Oh, er, right enough.'

With no one clamouring to take the show, it went quiet on the Tom Crean front for a while. And then in early 2003 I received a call out of the blue from a man who sounded either drunk or mad or both (he was neither). He was Ronan, the co-manager of a small Dublin venue called the New Theatre, a quirky seventy-seater space that had been built in the back of a communist bookshop in the middle of the city. I had almost forgotten that I'd phoned him weeks earlier and left a message about performing in his theatre. Ronan said he was sorry he hadn't got back to me, but that he had been in Cuba. He thought my show sounded fascinating so would I be interested in going to Dublin to perform some of it for him and his partner? I flew out there and did the first half of the show just for the two of them, which felt a wee bit odd. They certainly didn't rave about it, which, with hindsight, was possibly a shrewd business move on their part: appear too keen and you may give away your bargaining power. Nevertheless, they said they liked it and would like to book the show in their theatre. So we struck a deal, albeit not the best deal in the world for me: I would pay them rent and then once that rent had been paid we would split any seat sales 60–40 in their favour. I would start the run in September and it would be open-ended: I would just keep doing it as long as audiences wanted to see it. Not my finest negotiation financially, but I was desperate to get the show into Dublin and grateful that they wanted to take it.

In the meantime, I was offered a slot in the New York International Fringe Festival that summer. It was a trip that I would fund myself and I certainly would not make any money from it, but it had the potential to be a wonderful adventure and a chance to show Tom to a whole new audience. I arrived into JFK airport one warm August afternoon and was filled with anticipation as I was driven in a yellow cab across Brooklyn Bridge. How fantastic it was to experience New York, in all its Technicolor glory, for the very first time! Of course, me being me, along with the excitement came a lot of nervousness as I pondered whether the show would stand up on this side of the Atlantic. It was all very well in Ireland, in front of Tom's home crowd, but America was a whole other world. By way of warm-up for the Big Apple I had played the show at the Fuse Festival near my home in Medway in north Kent where it was very well received. I was pretty sure it would be okay, but this was New York and I was taking nothing for granted.

Once I had dropped off my cases in my swanky apartment overlooking the UN building (rented from a friend of a friend), I went along to meet my fellow performers at the festival's opening ceremony. Well, to call it an opening ceremony was a tad grand, if not a bit of an overstatement. I had been expecting wine, canapés, a hearty 'Oh you've come all the way from *Ireland* to do your show' acknowledgment and maybe some nice laminated badges showing our names and photos. What I got instead was a disparate group of hippies and odd-looking folk hanging about rather aimlessly in the foyer of an office block. None of us was introduced to one another but we were invited to walk across the road and stand in a park. It was at this point that I realised that this was Fringe Theatre with a capital F (for 'freaky'? 'Far out'? 'For feck's sake what have I left myself in for?'?!). A guy dressed all in black stood up and started talking about how important theatre was in giving people a voice. He had a roll of gaffer tape in his hand and we were each also given a piece of tape. As he spoke he started slowly wrapping the gaffer tape around his head, then before it went over his mouth and he lost the capacity to speak (see, the symbolism was not entirely lost on me, mystified as I was), he invited us all to put the tape over our mouths. At a given moment he would give a sign and then we would all rip off the tape in unison. We would not be silenced, we were artists and we would speak … Was this what I had signed up for? Some GCSE-type drama exercise? It didn't feel deep or meaningful, just ridiculous. Needless to say, I did not rip the tape from my mouth, valuing my skin just as much as my dignity.

Well, it was America. Rituals over, I was keen to see the theatre space I would be performing in. The festival was slightly under the radar and was taking place in a variety of spaces dotted all over Manhattan. My venue was in trendy Greenwich Village in the basement of a handsome red-brick building that was the home of a well-heeled arts lover. She had built the tiny theatre, complete with sixty seats and a bar, some five years earlier and it was a recognised venue on the fringe scene. I really liked it. I thought the intimate space would work well for my show and I could reassure myself that ten people would feel like a reasonable audience in such a small theatre. Much less pressure than trying to fill a 200-seater. I was sharing the space with several other companies and to be fair to everyone the performance times were rotated across afternoons and evenings. I was due to do five shows across the month-long festival. There was no dressing room as such, just a sort of corridor and it was filled with costumes from the other shows. I chose to get ready in the toilet for peace and privacy. Oh the glamour! But still, I was very excited to be there, in New York with my very own show and I was really looking forward to my first performance.

During the technical rehearsal, however, I hit upon a seemingly insurmountable problem. Up until that point I had always used a lamp onstage; it was a hurricane lamp with a candle and real flame inside and it held a very important significance in the play. For me, the candle represented life. So in the first half, after Scott is discovered dead, I blow out the candle to show the light of these men extinguished. 'Hmm, a naked flame on stage may be a problem,' said someone from the venue. I explained about the symbolism, but it cut no ice. I explained that the flame was always in my care and that a fire extinguisher would be standing by offstage, which had been good enough for theatres back home. But this, alas, was the United States, where only four months earlier, in Minnesota, around eighty people had been burned to death in a basement during a concert. No wonder they were being twitchy about my candle. Someone from the festival was summoned to assess the situation and he made his decision: I would not be having a naked flame on stage. And so I found myself trawling frantically around the shops of New York trying to find a battery-operated light, preferably (and you've got to love my blind optimism) one that had a shimmer like a candle. Nowadays, battery-operated lights are commonplace but they weren't a decade or so ago. Forget the shimmer, I couldn't even find a light. Eventually I found some battery stick lights that I stuck in the bottom of the lamp and I was able to operate by strapping an on/off switch underneath the lamp. Problem finally sorted, I was reminded of that army phrase: Adapt and Overcome …

I got ready nervously in the loo as my first show approached. Would I be on form, would the Americans understand me, would any audience actually turn up? I was delighted to see around twenty-five people when I walked out there. One of them was a reporter for the *Irish Voice* – an older man who loved the show – and we had a long chat afterwards. I did another show a couple of days later and all was going well until the day of the third performance. I was expecting a decent audience that night as I had a good time slot, an early evening one. As it turned out, I had no audience at all. At around 3 p.m. in the afternoon all the lights in my apartment suddenly went out. In fact, all the power seemed to have gone. I did not know if it was just my flat or more widespread. Bearing in mind that this was only a couple of years after the 9/11 atrocities, I felt uneasy. Was this another terrorist attack on New York? I went out into the corridor to try and find out what was happening but no one seemed to know. All the phones were off and I had no mobile in those days. I set off cautiously down the stairs and slowly made my way down in the pitch black from the fourth floor. In a shop I was told that there was a massive power cut across New York. Not a terrorist attack then. My relief was quickly superseded by my worries about the show that night. It was now 4 p.m. and I was due on stage in three hours. Someone else with more sense might have reasoned that, on this occasion, the show would not go on. People were saying that the blackout might have affected the whole of America (it hadn't). But even so, I thought that, by some miracle, my little basement theatre might possibly have some power, so I should go and see. Who says I'm not an optimist?

I walked for an hour and a half across town to the theatre as the subway was not running. The theatre was, of course, closed and no one else turned up. It seemed that I was the only one foolish enough to think that there would be any performances that evening. I waited for a good hour and when there was still no sign of life I decided to call it a night and walk over to Times Square to see what it looked like in the dark and without all of its trademark illuminations. As I made my way across powerless Manhattan, I saw people huddled round radios listening to the latest news, others drinking bottles of beer outside dark bars. Batteries were being sold, but not at inflated prices, and the atmosphere

DAILY ◉ NEWS

NEW YORK'S HOMETOWN NEWSPAPER

50¢   www.nydailynews.com   Friday, August 15, 2003

BLACKOUT

- 50 MILLION LOSE POWER
- CITY SWELTERS TO A HALT
- RUSH-HOUR CHAOS TODAY

The power blackout during the 2003 New York International
Fringe festival was front-page news.

was calm and good-natured. Outside Penn Station there were hundreds of stranded commuters. Times Square was unrecognisable without its neon hoardings and traffic and it was dotted with huge metal cans holding dancing flames. I bought some bottled water and went back to the flat, hoping that the next day would bring lights and loos (American toilets don't flush without electricity). But there was no power the next day. Well, not for us. In the true spirit of capitalism, the financial district was the first place to get its money-making power back. The rest of us had to wait another day, so I lost another performance from my precious five.

After these unexpected nights off, I now had three scheduled free days before my final two performances. I decided to fly over and see my sister Eithne in Toronto. Never physically robust, she was now very seriously ill and in hospital. Eithne is the second of my four older sisters and eight years older than me. We were not particularly close and, being so much younger, I hadn't had a lot to do with any of my elder siblings when I was growing up. But some things stick in my mind, particularly the torture that was my due as the youngest child of seven. My brother Raymond, for example, would put me in my duffle coat and hang me by the hood on the washing line, where I

Dooley delivers

By Joe Hurley
jhurley@irishecho.com

Galway-born actor explores
Crean's unique place in history

At age 40, despite patches of gray in his stubbly reddish-brown beard, here's enough childlike wonder remaining in Aidan Dooley's clear blue eyes to explain why he's such an effective storyteller, and why he manages, seemingly without effort, to maintain such a firm hold on his audiences.

The Galway-born actor's skill is abundantly obvious in "Tom Crean, Antarctic Explorer," the absorbing and illuminating one-man show he wrote and performs and which he brought to he massive 7th annual New York International Fringe Festival, currently underway and scheduled to continue hrough this coming Sunday at roughly twenty diverse venues scattered cross lower Manhattan.

Frank Hurley, and, very recently, a made-for-TV movie starring the Belfast-born actor Kenneth Branagh.

Crean, whose name is pronounced to rhyme with "clean," is the only individual to have served on all of these expeditions, only to be relegated to history's dustbin, a point wryly made by Dooley in his deeply informative and richly entertaining show. Actor Dooley is the youngest son of an avid amateur drummer who toured Ireland's towns and villages in the 1970s with a show band under the leadership of his brother, Maximilian.

"They had the whole thing, including music stands with the letters 'MD,' my uncle's initials, on

Aidan Dooley

Dooley's tale tells of one of the 20th entury's lost heroes, the uneducated d from Annascaul, Co. Kerry, who ined the Royal Navy when he was han three significant exploratory ventures, two under the leadership of obert Falcon Scott and the other with ir Ernest Shackleton on the RMS ndurance.

The Endurance story, which, unlike cott's second voyage, on the RMS erra Nova, ended happily, has been he subject of the motion picture South," utilizing the film and stills of he expedition's official photographer,

them," Dooley recalled.

Dealing eyeball to eyeball with audiences and dispensing information, sometimes masses of complicated, difficult information, is nothing new to Dooley, who has worked for a number of years with Spectrum Theatre Projects, developing various performance pieces on historical characters for all the National Museums in England.

"Tom Crean, Antarctic Explorer," in fact, began as a project Dooley worked up for the National Maritime Museum in Greenwich.

In addition, the actor and his wife, actress Miriam Cooper, operate a company called "Play on Words," which

tours Shakespeare and Living History shows to schools and small theaters all over the United Kingdom. The Shakespeare productions are very much reduced in scale. Their "Macbeth," for example, utilizes just three actors.

As if that regimen didn't keep Dooley sufficiently occupied, he and his wife also facilitate a Youth Theatre Project in the town of Rochester, Kent, where the couple and their two young children make their home. The Dooleys also somehow find time to operate Drama Summer Schools in Guernsey in the Channel Islands.

"In the year 2000, the Maritime Museum in Greenwich put on a big exhibition called 'South: the Race for the Pole,'" the actor said. "They were acquiring a lot of loan material from all sorts of places, from Norway, from the Scott Polar Institute and other venues. It was designed to be an 18-month show."

The museum had used actors before to enhance the displays, but this time there was a difference. "In the course of their research, they unearthed this Irish guy, this character who happened to have served as a Royal Navy crewman with both Scott and Shackleton," he said.

Dooley referred, of course, to Robert Falcon Scott and Sir Ernest Shackleton, the most celebrated figures in the history of British polar exploration.

"There were two other men, who got more polar medals than Crean did, because they went on more voyages. They were the Joyce twins, and I think they were Irish, too. They went on four expeditions altogether, but under different leaders," Dooley added.

The polar ventures were known by the names of their ships, first the RMS Explorer and the RMS Terra Nova, both captained by Scott, and then the RMS Endurance, with Shackleton in command.

"Actually, Shackleton had made a voyage earlier than the Endurance," he said. "That was the Nimrod in 1909, where Shackleton got within 90 miles of the Pole, and then turned back because two of his men were ill. That was where Shackleton got his knighthood, because he got so close."

When asked why he'd turned back, Shackleton had a ready answer: "Isn't it better to be a living donkey than a dead lion?"

"That's indicative of what Shackleton was like, I think," Dooley said. "The point the museum wanted Crean to make was to show visitors to the exhibition just how different Scott and Shackleton were from each other. He was only a conduit for that point of

view, in the mind of the museum."

At this point, a writer named Michael Smith wrote a book, "Unsung Hero," telling Crean's story and the adventuring Kerryman came out from the shadows, if only somewhat.

Dooley's museum performances require slightly different acting skills from those he might be required to come up with in more conventional theatrical circumstances.

"Every museum we work in has its own style," he said. "Sometimes we work in the galleries, wearing costumes and demonstrating things, and interacting directly with the visitors."

At one point, Dooley found himself playing Thomas Crapper, and demonstrating the "flushometer," which Crapper is widely believed to have invented, even though he never took out a patent on it.

Dooley's acting career has by no means been confined to his museum and instructional work. In 1992, he appeared in a revival of Brian Friel's "Philadelphia, Here I Come." The production started at the King's Head Pub in Islington, and was successful enough to warrant a transfer to Wyndham's Theatre in the West end, where it ran for four months.

"It was when 'Dancing at Lughnasa' was flying high and everyone was interested in Friel," he recalled. "We got amazing reviews, and I had four months of absolute bliss because Friel's writing is so rich. I had a great time on the West End stage. I was only on stage for something like ten minutes, playing the small role of Tom, one of the hero's friends, but I never ever got bored. I met Friel once when he came to theater in the last week," he said. "I must have been like a slobbering groupie."

Aidan Dooley had graduated from "The Bish" in Galway, that being the informal name by which St. Joseph's College is known, because it had been a Bishops' Monastery or something of the kind.

"It was just a day school, not a posh boarding school or anything like that," he said. "I'd become involved in amateur dramatics by that time, but there weren't any actual drama schools in Ireland at the time. So I ended up working for Allied Irish Bank in Dublin as a clerk."

In 1985, Dooley asked the bank to transfer him to London, because he thought he could at least take drama courses in night school. He found himself working in Cricklewood, which he calls "the 33rd county," because of the large number of Irish who live there and in Kilburn, the adjacent area of North London.

After two years, he left the bank and enrolled in drama school in Guildford full time. He could only afford a single year there.

It happened that, when his tenure at Guildford ended, a new museum, the Museum of the Moving Image, opened in London. The MOMI director decided to use actors and Dooley was one of them.

"I did a whole year there and I learned a lot," he recalled. "I learned how to deal with people, and how to create audiences in those environments in which people are just passing through. I learned how to catch people and keep them entertained, and how not to catch them if they didn't want to

See DELIVERS, Page 26

The *Irish Echo* report on Aidan's appearance in the New York Fringe Festival, August 2003.

would dangle until someone took pity on me. I also remember my sisters putting me in the gusset of my mother's tights and whizzing me around as a kind of human mop – they were actually using me and the tights to clean the lino floors. For me, that's a very funny, warm image. Once I told this story at a dinner party not long after I started going out with Miriam, expecting everyone to laugh. Nobody did. Lost in translation maybe. Beyond the mam's tights story, I don't much remember Eithne being in the house at all, though I seem to remember that she sold Mary Quant perfume in a department store. When I say we weren't close, it was due purely to the age difference and the size of our family. There were so many of us that it was almost a relief when someone moved out and we had a bit more space.

Eithne lived in Toronto with her husband and two daughters. I had spent a happy summer there when I was fifteen but had not been back since.

I wished now that I wasn't seeing her in such sad circumstances. My mother was already there, nursing her. Fidelma, our eldest sister, was flying in from Australia. This was to be my last visit, not that I knew it at the time. I went to the hospital to see her and was shocked at how ill she looked, how frail. But Eithne had managed to fight off some serious illnesses previously so I could not believe that she

The entire Dooley family together in 1993: *back row (l–r)*: Eithne, Ann Marie, Raymond, mother Ellen (known as Nellie), Fidelma, father Jimmy, Gerard; *front row (l–r)*: Aidan and Ursula.

would not do so again. We could see Eithne was very sick but it was only my mother who knew she was dying. Mam decided, for better or worse, that it would be better, kinder, not to tell Eithne the bleak truth. I spent the night in Eithne's house with my mam and sister and then had to fly back to New York. When I said goodbye to Eithne, I couldn't hug her because it hurt her too much. I told her to keep fighting. 'I don't know if I have the strength to fight this one,' she said. I must have felt that she would summon the strength from somewhere, just as she always had, but she died three months later. When I reflect on this time, I am struck by my mother's devoted care for my sister. This was a mother's commitment to her child – one of her babies, no matter what her age, and a baby she was going to lose. Unimaginable for any mother. For several months, she sat each and every day by Eithne's hospital bed, comforting her and just being there with her. Quite frankly, I marvel at the immensity of my mother's love when, tenderly caring for her dying daughter, she must have been going through the worst possible pain herself.

I flew back to New York to do my last two performances and they went well. I averaged about thirty people per show so it always felt I was playing to a decent-sized audience. There were no standing ovations but the response was very positive. Apart from a thrilling life experience, I came away from New York with two major marketing tools: a five-star review from yer man who came to the first night (no other journalists attended) and, unbeknown to me, an award for the Best Solo Show. I didn't hear about the award until I arrived home, didn't even know I was up for it. To tell the truth, I could have been the only solo show in the whole festival, who knows? The important thing for me was that I had

Unsung polar hero

Dooley brings alive the Kerryman who aided Scott and Shackleton

A Kerryman named Tom Crean played a role in the life and work of both Captain Robert Falcon Scott and Sir Ernest Shackleton, very similar to the parts performed in "Hamlet" by Rosencrantz and Guildenstern, schoolboy friends of the Prince of Denmark.

Like those background characters in Shakespeare's most durable tragedy, Crean was always part of the action when those celebrated British scientists and adventurers were trying to conquer the Antarctic, but he never became famous and remains, to this day, something of an overlooked footnote, if that, in the troubled history of polar exploration.

Crean's anonymousness is all the more surprising in the face of the fact that he alone took part in all three of the period's most significant British exploratory ventures.

Born in 1877, he joined the Royal Navy at 15 and served on HMS Discovery from 1901-04, on Terra Nova from 1910-13, both under Scott, and on Endurance, on the expedition headed by Shackleton from 1914-16.

Crean would probably remain forev-

On the Aisle

Joseph Hurley
jhurley@irishecho.com

Tom Crean, Antarctic Explorer
Written by: Aidan Dooley
Starring: Aidan Dooley
Where: Fat Chance Productions' Ground Floor, 312 West 11th St., NYC
When: Four performances remaining.

The lowdown:
An ingenious one-man show commemorates a man who deserves to be more than a historical footnote.

er a shadow figure were it not for Michael Smith's biography, "Unsung Hero," which was one of the primary sources, not to mention inspirations, for "Tom Crean, Antarctic Explorer," the

extraordinary one-man show written and performed by Galway-born actor Aidan Dooley, and being performed as part of the 7th New York International Fringe Festival, which began last Friday and continues all over Lower Manhattan through Aug. 24.

Speaking directly and, for the most part, gently to his audience, the shyly humorous and self-effacing Dooley presents an easily digested mini-history of the British adventures and misadventures in which Crean took part and which consumed so much of his life between the ages of 24 and 39, when he came back from the Endurance voyage.

At the same time, in his charmingly understated way, Dooley both subtly impersonates Crean and "demonstrates" the primitive and often inadequate equipment with which Shackleton and his colleagues had to equip the expedition.

As he dons, one after another, the items worn by Shackleton and the others, "distressed" garments that look almost alarmingly real, Dooley, at moments, very nearly approaches resembling a package, or a heap of equipment left behind at base camp and rediscovered decades later.

When Scott divided his party and

See **FRINGE**, Page 32

Great review in New York City from *The Irish Echo*, 13 August 2003.

won an award, and in America, no less. With the Dublin gig coming up this would stand me in very good stead. There's nothing like a foreign accolade to make Ireland take you seriously as an artist.

I didn't, in the end, do an open-ended run at the New Theatre as agreed with manager Ronan. He had phoned me a few weeks before to say that he had another show coming into the theatre after mine, so would it be all right for me to do just a three-week run? It actually suited me better to be committed for a shorter time, given the unfavourable financial deal we had made. On the plus side, the theatre agreed to promote the show and they employed a wonderful PR woman, Carmel White, who has since died, sadly. She put out press releases about this exciting new play that had won an award in New York and, using her fantastic contacts, she got me TV and press interviews. It meant my Dublin run was starting with a big momentum. Another factor in my favour was the timing of the run. I was coming into the theatre in the middle of September when everyone was getting ready for the Dublin Theatre and Fringe festival, which begins in early October. In other words, there was very little happening on stage and precious few shows opening in mid September – apart from mine.

This is no doubt the reason why, on my first night, all the big names from the Irish press turned out. One of these was Emer O'Kelly from the *Sunday Independent* who had a reputation for making or breaking a show depending on whether or not she warmed to it. No pressure then! Luckily I didn't know beforehand that the heavyweight reviewers were all out in force. I was nervous enough as it was, because this was the first time I had performed the whole show in a theatre for many weeks and I was still a bit shaky on the second half. I just had to trust that it would come back to me.

My dressing room was little more than an outdoor shack, warmed by a Calor gas heater and with an old mirror propped up against a wall. Its lack of comforts, I told myself, would help me prepare mentally for my story of physical deprivation. I knew it was an important night for me and the show. But the truth was that I had not performed the second half of the show, the Shackleton story, for about a year, when I had done my first little tour in Ireland. In New York during the summer, I had concentrated solely on the first half of the play, the Scott story. And here's the thing, I still hadn't written down the script: it was all in my head. The first half of the play was tight because I knew it very well but the second half was much less honed. I knew the story more or less and had a rough structure but I wouldn't really know what would come out of my mouth until I was on that stage. Maybe it says something about my mental make-up that I didn't want to start going over the second half in my head before the show but I knew that, without an audience, it wouldn't all flow – I somehow needed the adrenaline to bring out the story. I just had to go on stage and trust that Tom would take me where I needed to go.

And there was plenty of adrenaline on that Wednesday night. The house was packed. I had no idea how many journalists were out there, which was probably just as well. It was one of those magical nights that, as an actor, you know will happen rarely in your career, when there's a particular alchemy between you and that audience, between you and the play. Everything just worked and had a kind of dangerous fizz that would never be repeated. I felt it, even before the audience erupted at the end of the show and stood on their feet, clapping wildly and cheering. It was an unforgettable moment for me. The reviews came out on the Sunday. I know we actors say reviews don't matter, and they shouldn't, but the really good ones and the really bad ones stay with you for a long time. I suppose I could have just not read them, but I had to know, no matter how painful the words. Good reviews could really help me promote the show. But what if they were bad? This was my show, conceived, written, directed and acted by me, so there was no way not to take criticism personally.

I remember going to the shop and buying all of the papers and thinking, 'Oh God, here we go.' I was amazed. They weren't just good reviews: they were extraordinary. They were so good that I sat and cried. I phoned Miriam in England and told her that they could not have been more glowing if I had written them myself. Modesty prevents me from quoting any of the accolades apart from

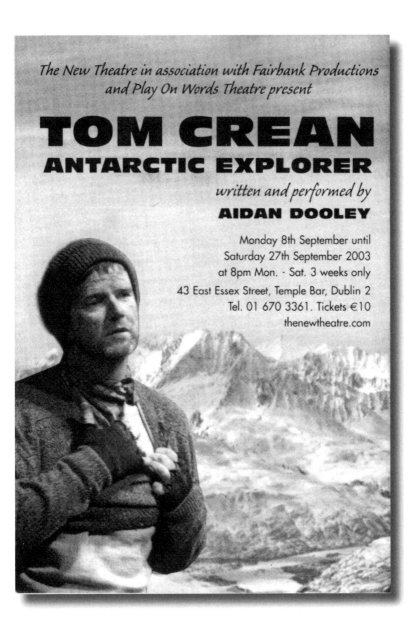

Poster advertising the New Theatre run of *Tom Crean – Antarctic Explorer* in September 2003.

one critic who really touched me when she wrote that my performance 'gives everything and asks for nothing'. All these superlatives from respected critics boosted my artistic confidence hugely and I knew they would help me take the show further. Who cares if I didn't know how I was going to pay the mortgage next month? They liked it! They loved it! I was elated.

Thanks to the reviews and word of mouth, my four-week run at the New Theatre was a sell-out. Cousins I'd not seen in years phoned to see if I could get them tickets. I wasn't used to doing the show for such a long run and became utterly exhausted. Backstage, I would lie down on three hard kitchen chairs and fall asleep at the drop of a hat. Weirdly, I often did really good shows when I was very tired because they had a calm clarity to them. I didn't do much post-show carousing, but would usually go back to my friend John's house in Harold's Cross where I was staying and, over a takeaway, would analyse my performance that night: what had worked, what hadn't and why. Halfway through the run, I decided, finally, that it would be a good idea to write down the script. This caused much surprise – and consternation – for the theatre manager. He came into the dressing room while I was scribbling away before the show one

Crean's humour and generosity brought to life

THEATRE
EMER O'KELLY

TO MAKE someone of unadventurous spirit understand why others can undertake extraordinary adventures that try and test them beyond what most of us could even contemplate enduring is an immense achievement of description and imagination. And that is what Aidan Dooley has done with his *Tom Crean, Antarctic Explorer*.

He makes us understand the spirit of the adventurous

and heroic madmen, who like Sir Edmund Hillery with Everest, "do it because it's there." And in Crean's time they did it without the assistance of communications technology. To be stranded in danger meant fearful isolation without hope of rescue, and only the prospect of a lingering and painful death.

The play is presumably the first piece of writing from the London-based Irish actor, and it's an extraordinary presentation. It's at the New Theatre in Essex Street in Dublin,

produced there in conjunction with Fairbank and Play on Words, and, apart from its technical excellence and hidden intensity of acting, it is a hymn of revelation and generosity.

How much of the characterisation of Tom Crean, the Royal Navy rating from Kerry who went to Antarctica three times, twice with Scott and once with Ernest Shackleton, is based on fact, and how much is literary and dramatic licence is not clear, since the man apparently left no diaries and accounts of his strange life and times. But what Dooley gives us is a man of unsurpassed humour and generosity, ready to give credit to decency and heroism wherever he finds it. There is no class bitterness, no chip on the shoulder, no begrudgery

ADVENTURER: Aiden Dooley as Tom Crean

against comrades who fell short of the required level of superhuman courage and grit. Dooley's Crean talks of being granted the "honour" of breaking open the ice-bound tent to discover the dead bodies of Scott and his colleagues, after the body-breaking and spirit-testing rescue mission back from base camp in the arid hope of rescuing them.

He gives us a *Boys' Own* hero; but one adults can believe in, to inspire us when the going gets tough and the human spirit fails. It's a remarkable and uplifting piece of theatre, gives everything, and asks nothing.

A glowing *Sunday Independent* review of Aidan's performance in the New Theatre, September 2003.

evening and asked me what I was doing. I told him I was writing the second half of the show. 'What?' he gasped. 'You are packing out the theatre every night and you are only just writing it? Jaysus …'

Despite the success of the show, I didn't end up making much money. It was a sharp lesson and my business acumen improved after this experience. But what's money when you are flushed with critical success? More importantly, I came away from Dublin with some new tour dates to venues I wouldn't previously have ever have dreamed of getting into, including the Town Hall theatre in Galway and the Civic Theatre in Tallaght, in south County Dublin. I was also booked to perform the show at Glór, a music venue in County Clare.

Despite my success at the New Theatre, I still dreamed of playing a big Dublin venue. One night, as I stood outside the New Theatre after the show, enjoying the balmy September evening, I could hear the sounds of the audience in the nearby Olympia Theatre. One of the biggest theatres in Ireland, the Olympia held special memories for me. I saw Galway's fantastic Druid Theatre perform there and I especially remember a production of *The Playboy of the Western World* by Ballet Ireland that had The Chieftains playing live in the pit. The Chieftains! And as I stood there, hearing the sound of the Olympia audience, I tried to imagine what it would be like to play to an audience of 1,200 instead of the ninety who filled up the New Theatre every night. Taking Tom to a venue like the Olympia was, of course, a dream that I could never seriously expect to come true. Could I?

8
THE LUCK OF THE IRISH

That man up there, I'm telling ya he's looking after me.

From *Tom Crean – Antarctic Explorer* (Aidan Dooley)

Courage, determination, the ability to stay cool under pressure: these are character traits that undoubtedly contributed towards Tom Crean's outstanding achievements in the South Pole. But sometimes a hero needs sheer luck on his side. During the *Terra Nova* expedition, Crean, Henry Bowers and Apsley Cherry-Garrard were returning to Hut Point from a depot-laying expedition when they became stranded on an ice floe. With the sea ice breaking up all around them, the men were floating out to certain death on the open sea and the situation seemed hopeless. All they could do was leap from one ice floe to another, dragging their sledges and frightened ponies with them, in the hope that they would find a substantial piece of ice that might carry them to the safety of the ice shelf itself. Known as the Ross Ice Shelf or Great Ice Barrier, this ice shelf is hundreds of feet thick, ending in an almost vertical cliff face, up to 160 feet high, on its oceanward side. In the midst of this treacherous situation, it was Tom Crean who took charge and kept the other, less experienced men calm. Even when killer whales started to circle them, Tom remained composed. After six terrifying hours on the broken ice, it was Tom who volunteered to try and get help. They were now close to the Barrier. His plan was to leap from one floe to another to get close enough to the Barrier to climb onto it and ascend its 20ft sheer face. It was another one of those desperate do-or-die plans. At any point, Tom could have fallen into the freezing water, or been attacked by a killer whale. Even if he made it onto the Barrier, he then had to try and climb its steep cliff with just a ski stick. Crean, as always, kept his cool, waited patiently for a sturdy floe to take him to the Barrier and then managed to scramble up it and raise the alarm. His heroic efforts to save his comrades earned much praise from Scott. You could say that, with his immense courage and fortitude,

Crean made his own luck. On the other hand, he was also fortunate that a killer whale didn't fancy him for lunch.

When I am onstage as Tom, there is one small part of my costume that the audience never notices but that I wouldn't ever be without. Around my neck I wear a pair of scapulars, which – for those who don't know – are prayers written on a piece of cloth and tied around my neck with a thin piece of leather. Tom would have been given his scapulars as a young Catholic lad, perhaps around the time of his confirmation, and he never went anywhere without them. We have no idea which prayers Tom carried with him but they were his talisman, giving him the sense that he was being protected and watched over. And when you consider just how many times he managed to elude the jaws of death, he must have felt at certain moments that some higher power was definitely on his side.

It was lucky that Tom joined the Royal Navy. It was a good job, a job for life, which would have been a very rare thing in those volatile days of the late Victorian period when a young working-class lad might struggle to find a job and could easily find himself in the workhouse if he stepped out of line. Even if you were lucky enough to be taken on by the navy in the first place, you only had a one in ten chance of staying in it beyond the first six months as all the weaker candidates were gradually weeded out. In the navy, as on the ice, only the strong survived.

But in the Antarctic, no man, not even the strongest, bravest man, is a match for Mother Nature should she choose to unleash her unholy powers. That's where you need a little bit of luck. On 18 February 1912, when Tom Crean set off on his solo journey to save the life of Lieutenant Evans and Bill Lashly, it was his astonishing strength of character that drove him on when he had almost reached the limits of his endurance. As he steadily put one foot in front of the other and kept moving despite unimaginable exhaustion, he could see a storm gathering. All he could do was hope that the bad weather held off until he reached safety. And, miraculously, it did. Within thirty minutes of Tom arriving at Hut Point, an almighty blizzard descended that was so intense, it delayed the rescue of Evans and Lashly by a day and a half. Had Tom's punishing journey taken just half an hour longer, no amount of courage would have saved him or the two men clinging on to life in that little tent. They would most certainly have perished.

The weather was also on Tom's side when he, Shackleton and Worsley crossed South Georgia in order to save their comrades stranded on Elephant Island. Before the trio set off on their near-impossible journey, they were forced to wait a couple of days for the appalling weather conditions to abate. When they finally set off, in the early hours of 19 May 1918, it was a fine clear night. And conditions remained calm for the thirty-six hours it took them to make their weary, sleepless way across the untrodden peaks and glaciers of South Georgia. Not long after the men staggered into the whaling station at Stromness, the weather closed in and a blizzard erupted. Once again the weather had been kind at a crucial moment. All three men said afterwards that, during their journey, they each had the curious and private sensation that there was a fourth person with them. Shackleton and Worsley both wrote about the experience. Tom simply said, some years later, 'The Lord brought us home.' This sense of otherness could have been delirium born out of sleep deprivation, but it is certainly very odd that each of the men felt that another presence was there with them. God? Lady Luck? The spirit of all those explorers who had not been so lucky?

When I travelled to South Georgia, and looked up at the jagged outlines of those astonishingly sheer mountain ranges, I couldn't help but marvel at how those men survived. How did Crean,

Shackleton and Worsley manage to negotiate their way through those serrated precipices without proper equipment? Who was watching over them when they slid down one of those near-vertical cliffs in the dark on a makeshift sledge? No wonder Tom believed he was being protected by a higher power.

Luck has also played a part in the success of my play. It was certainly fortunate that the year after I first started touring the show, there was a Guinness advertisement featuring none other than Tom. In the advertisement, Tom the explorer is trudging through the Antarctic snow and dreaming of the future, of the creamy pints that he will be serving in his own pub, the South Pole Inn. Such is the power of television and advertising that it brought Tom into the Irish consciousness. When I first did the character of Tom in the museums in 2001, the only Irish people who had heard of him and who would come up to talk to me about him were from Kerry. There would be Irish folk from Galway, Donegal and all over Ireland who at that time had never heard of him. Then, thanks to Michael Smith's biography *An Unsung Hero* (read it if you haven't already: it's fantastic) and this advertisement, more and more people became aware of Tom.

After my stint at the New Theatre in Dublin, I did a couple of tours of Ireland and was gradually building up audiences. Venue managers were telling me that they were seeing people in their theatres who had never been inside before, men in their forties and fifties, perhaps walkers and climbers who had read Michael's book and had a keen interest in polar exploration. Despite my modest and growing success with the show, I really wanted to get into a big theatre in Dublin so I could reach more people and get Tom's story out to a more established theatre audience – and maybe also earn a few bob into the bargain. It was in 2005 that I had another lucky break that would launch me into Dublin. I was playing at the Civic Theatre in Tallaght, a 300-seater in south County Dublin. It is run by a lovely woman called Bríd Dukes who has been a loyal supporter of the show and had me back many times over the years. This was, I think, my third visit to the Civic. Prompted by my close friend Eileen, I asked Bríd a very important question: 'If I only had six months left to do this show and wanted to attract the biggest audiences possible, who's the one person in Ireland that should see it?' Bríd said, without hesitation, 'Pat Moylan.' A very influential producer, she ran the Andrews Lane Theatre in Dublin with Breda Cashe. Pat was the driving force behind some huge theatre hits including *Stones in His Pockets*. Bríd phoned up Pat then and there and said, 'You need to come see Aidan Dooley's show. It has the potential to be another *Alone It Stands*.' Bríd was referring to a play about the Munster rugby team beating the All Blacks that had really captured the public's imagination a few years earlier. So, despite being very busy with two other shows, Pat came to see me perform at the Civic Theatre one Saturday night. She loved it and booked me to play at Andrews Lane in spring 2006. Here was a fantastically lucky break: Pat Moylan was on board.

Timing, as they say, is all and my second piece of serendipity came that spring. I was a few days into the run at Andrews Lane Theatre. The venue seated 250 people and I was doing okay, gradually building up audiences to over 150, which was fine by me. On the Friday of the first week, Pat had arranged a radio interview for me to plug the show. Little did I know what a catalyst this would be! I was a guest on RTÉ's Derek Mooney programme, a chat show that had been running for about six months and had become pretty popular. He had different themes and guests every week. I was on with an ornithologist and a walker who had both, by chance, seen my show. I performed an excerpt on air and I was pleased that the radio show was live because it meant that they could not edit my performance as has happened on other, pre-recorded radio interviews and which never works as well as hearing a whole chunk in full flow. After my little turn, I chatted on air to Derek and his guests about the play. The walker raved about it, at which point the switchboard literally lit up and people were calling in from Cork and Galway and all over Ireland to say they'd seen my play and how fantastic it was. I couldn't have hoped for better publicity, or endorsement of my work. When I think about it, the show was on at a peak time on a Friday afternoon, when people may have been in the car, picking up the children from school, or driving home early from the office to start the weekend. Timing, you see. The irony was that after all the on-air talk about the show, I was nearly late for that night's performance as the taxi that was supposed to take me from the radio station back into town never materialised.

By the beginning of the following week the show was totally sold out for the remaining month. I was delighted. So was Pat, who asked me to return with it in October. She also was responsible for another important milestone in the life of my play because she helped bring it to the Edinburgh Fringe Festival that August, in 2006. Performing in the Edinburgh Fringe is a manic, mad, marvellous experience. As everyone who has performed there knows, getting a decent venue and time slot is essential. There are so many acts and shows vying for audiences that you need to maximise your chances of getting bums on seats. You don't want to be one of the poor, bleary-eyed souls performing at 9 a.m. to two people and a dog, nor do you want to be in an out-of-the-way, anonymous room that has suddenly become a theatre space for three weeks in August. I was fortunate. Thanks to Pat, I had bagged a nice 100-seater studio in the high-profile Assembly Rooms and I had a good mid-afternoon slot. Even so, there are no guarantees in Edinburgh. That's why the Royal Mile, Princes Street and every other thoroughfare are always teeming with people proffering flyers, dressed in strange costumes, stilt walking and carrying out other attention-seeking activities. Reviews help, of course (as long as they're good, obviously), but for unknown artists, the best way to get people through the door is to win a coveted Fringe First Award. This is a prestigious prize, given out only to pieces of new writing and, as far as Edinburgh audiences are concerned, it's a real game changer.

I would be lying if I said that I hadn't dreamed about winning a Fringe First. Up to that point, I'd had such a great response from press and audiences that I dared to think I might be in with a small chance. This hope was soon dashed when, four days into the run, I got a nice review in *The Scotsman*. But the reviewer gave the show four stars and I knew from talking to people that you're not in with a chance for a Fringe First unless you get five stars. Well, at least now I knew not to hold out any false hope. One of the worst shows I ever did at Edinburgh was early on when I thought the *Daily Mail* were in to review me. I tried far too hard and it spoiled the rhythm and integrity of my performance. So, lessons learned. Forget about reviews and prizes: just do the show for the audiences who have paid to come to see you. And I did. I relaxed, told Tom's story and I got into this wonderful, rare groove where I felt the show was the best it could be. Sometimes I would come off stage and think, 'how can I capture this performance so that every show is as good as this?'

Each show in the Fringe is given a strict time allocation and you cannot run over or it will affect the show coming in straight after you. I had to do a 75-minute version of my two-hour show, with no interval and so had to decide which cuts to make. But I wouldn't know if I had got the timing right until I tried it in performance. There was no point in my trying to time it on my own beforehand: I couldn't just rattle it off without an audience. So, during the show, I had people at the back of the theatre sending me signals with a torch at the fifty-

THE SCOTSMAN
Fringe Awards

The Scotsman would like to invite

Tom Crean — Antarnic Explorer

to The Scotsman Fringe Awards,
at 11am on Friday 25 August 2006
at the Assembly Rooms, George Street

10.45am To be seated in Music Hall
Reception in Fremantle Media Club bar after show
Please bring this invitation with you

RSVP
Andrew Eaton
Arts Editor
aeaton@scotsman.com

The invitation to receive the Fringe First Award at the Edinburgh
Fringe Festival, August 2006.

minute mark and then the hour, so I knew whether I needed to speed up, slow down, take out an extra bit so that I didn't run over. Gradually, I paced myself perfectly for the seventy-five minutes.

During the second week of the run, someone from the Assembly Rooms brought me a piece of most unexpected news: I had won a Fringe First. I couldn't believe it but I was absolutely elated, especially because I felt the show had never been better than it was at that moment. Then everything changed. Suddenly, the show was sold out. You couldn't get a ticket for love nor money. It was crazy. I was on the six o'clock news in Ireland – 'Irish play wins Fringe First in Edinburgh.' People who had gone to school with me were phoning up and all the press wanted to interview me. I was a hit! Many doors opened for me after Edinburgh and the following eighteen months were a thrilling, intense rollercoaster that took me all over the world.

First stop was back in Dublin for a second run at Andrews Lane that October and I arrived with Pat Moylan's publicity team in full swing, fresh from the success of Edinburgh. During the run at Andrews Lane, I was given a slot on RTÉ's TV show *The Panel*, hosted by Dara Ó Briain, which was an Irish version of the BBC's *Mock the Week*. Celebrity panellists, often comedians, had a humorous chat about topical news stories and then they would wheel out a guest or two, like me. I was going to talk about the show and was wondering how I would keep up with the razor-sharp wit of Ó Briain and the likes of Ed Byrne who was on the panel that week. I knew there would be time before the show to meet everyone and to outline roughly the content of our chat. The weather, however, had other plans. A terrible storm disrupted all the flights that day, meaning that Dara and his panel got to the studio only about half an hour before the live show, so we all had to busk it. I had expected that they might make a few jokes at my expense – you never really know what to expect from that sort of show. But in the event, they went quite lightly on me, talked about Scott and Shackleton and I managed to hold my own. I even enjoyed the experience. You could say that appearing on TV chat shows had long been a fantasy of mine ever since the days as an eleven-year-old boy walking home from school when I used to dream about being interviewed by Gay Byrne on *The Late Late Show*. I never got to be interviewed by him on that show but I did get to meet the man himself in an incident that I shall refer to as The Night Gay Byrne Saw Me in My Underpants.

It happened during one of the most extraordinary weeks in the story of my show. It was the week that kicked off an amazing year for me and Tom Crean. When Pat Moylan had first suggested that I should take Tom to the Olympia Theatre, I laughed out loud. That was back in April 2006 and I had just finished my first sell-out run at Andrews Lane. Pat said that the Olympia had a free week the following January and she thought I should grab it. I actually said to her, 'Pat, you're f***ing mad. An unknown actor in a relatively unknown story and you're wanting to put me in a thousand-seater theatre, not just for a night but for a whole week?' Pat said, 'Yes, I think it will do really well.' And if Pat believed in it, then I knew it wasn't a totally mad idea. As a formidable business woman, Pat has a nose for a smash hit. It was Pat who, along with Breda Cashe, found *Alone It Stands*, and *I, Keano* (the hit musical about Roy Keane leaving the Irish football team before the 2002 World Cup). It was Pat who found the hit play *Stones in His Pockets*. And it was Pat who created the Andrews Lane Theatre and then sold it at the height of the Celtic Tiger. She knew her stuff all right. She could not have achieved any of this without being a tough negotiator. If we were moving into the big league, I didn't want anyone, least of all Pat, to forget that it was my show, that my heart and soul were invested in it, not to mention years of hard graft. Deciding to lay my cards on the table,

The poster for Aidan's 2013 show in the front window of the Olympia Theatre's box office.

I looked her square in the eye and said to her: 'Pat, I cannot do this show if I feel I'm not getting my fair share.' She replied, 'I understand.' And that was that. We had an understanding, which has always been honoured. And so it came to pass, in January 2007, I played the Olympia Theatre in Dublin for the first time.

In December 2006, Pat phoned me at home in Rochester to say that with a month still to go, half the Olympia tickets had been sold. By the time I arrived the following January, all the seats had sold out. I couldn't believe it: 1,200 people in every audience for six nights and a matinee. I remember arriving at the theatre and stepping onto the stage for the first time.

I felt quite overcome by the sheer scale of it and the sense of history. Looking up at the circle and higher levels, it seemed to me that the rows of seats went on forever. After being on tour, I was used to adapting the show for whatever space I was in but I had never played any space quite as large as this. I usually like to be near the audience because it's quite an intimate piece of storytelling, but at the Olympia I had to position myself further back so that everyone could see me. I was worrying about the sightlines for people way up in the gods and wondering if I needed to go back even further, when someone quipped, 'They only paid twenty euros – don't worry about them!' Oh, but I did. However, you can only do what you can do. I had to hope that my instinct to play the space would kick in and that I would somehow reach everyone in that vast auditorium. I remember an invaluable piece of advice I was given when *Philadelphia, Here I Come!* transferred from a small pub theatre to the West End. A friend of mine, George Heslin, advised me that, when you go to a bigger stage, you don't *act* bigger, you *think* bigger. So that's what I tried to do, to see the pictures bigger and more vividly. I also had some rifle mikes at the end of the stage to push out the sound to the back of the auditorium.

I did a preview on the Monday, which went well, and opening night was really the Tuesday. My family had come up from Galway and we had dinner before the show. My parents had seen it many times by this point but never in such a huge, well-known venue. My sister Ann Marie had texted me before they arrived in Dublin to say how excited they were. As I was in the dressing room getting ready, the stage manager came in and said, 'Aidan, I've worked in the theatre for many years and I have never heard what I have just heard: ticket touts asking if anyone had spare tickets for a show!' The place was buzzing and, with all that weight of expectation, it would have been so easy to succumb to nerves. But the way I coped was to remind myself of my genuine belief that I am just a conduit for Tom: it's his story, not mine. I always keep a firm hold on that rope because it keeps me grounded. On that opening night at the Olympia, I actually didn't feel at all overwhelmed by the size of the theatre. The audience did not seem too far away and I felt able to speak to them directly and make contact with them just as I would do in a tiny studio space. The only difference was that I couldn't see their faces. Afterwards, I had an amazing response. I felt proud and humble at the same time. I make sure Tom always takes a bow after a show. I leave my hat on and bow as Tom and then take it off to take a curtain call as Aidan the actor. A small but significant detail and even if no else notices, it is my homage to Tom.

I was so glad that my parents were there to see that performance. Afterwards there was a little party laid on with food and wine. My dad, as usual, pointed out the bits I had missed out that I shouldn't have missed out because they were his favourites. He was also giving out to an Irish fella at the party who had been snooker world champion a few years earlier but who had recently lost a couple of big matches. All in all, a grand, unforgettable night.

The rest of the Olympia run went well, standing ovations every time. One night there was a knock on my dressing-room door after the show. Backstage at the Olympia is a bit of a rabbit warren, with twisting Victorian staircases that lead eventually to the dressing room. Not an easy place to find and the only person who ever came to my room was the stage manager. So when I heard a knock I assumed it was him and I told him to come in. Having stripped off my sweaty costume I was sitting there in my underpants. Imagine my horror when the door opened to reveal none other than Gay Byrne, his wife and two friends. My wife, Miriam, who was there with me, handed me my trousers and I was so busy scrambling into them that I couldn't extend the hand of hospitality to say, 'Come in, welcome!' I really wanted to tell Gay how glad I was to meet him and how much of an impact his TV show had had on me as a youngster. During the 1970s, *The Late Late Show* was just about the only Irish TV programme that discussed openly topics such as divorce and women's liberation. In a land ruled by Rome, it was brave and controversial to tackle such issues and I admired him heartily for it. Gay really liked my show. He had seen it a couple of times before this and had talked about it on his radio programme. Seeing my disarray in the dressing room he tactfully said that no, he wouldn't stay, he just wanted to say how much he'd enjoyed the performance, and then he beat a gentle retreat. So there it was, the moment I'd dreamed of as a schoolboy: I met Gay Byrne. In my underpants.

My week at the Olympia boosted the status of the show. The fact that I had sold out one of the biggest, best-known theatres in Dublin was invaluable. Word of mouth got round and my stock went up. I have played the Olympia numerous times since that January in 2007 and each time there is an advertisement for the show on the back page of *The Irish Times*. It feeds the publicity for my Irish tours because by the time I get to, say, Thurles, the venue is full partly because people have seen the advert in the national newspaper.

There was another reason why that week was so incredible to me: it earned me more security than I could have ever dreamed possible. I walked away from the Olympia with the equivalent of several years' museum wages. This was serious, life-changing money for anyone, but for a theatre actor it was nothing short of a miracle. After all those years of scrimping, worrying and trying to eke out a living from our precarious profession, Miriam and I could finally breathe. I arrived home from that tour knowing we were financially secure

In 2007, Aidan travelled so much that his then seven-year-old daughter Nancy wrote to say she missed him.

for a good while. We no longer had to worry about how we would pay the mortgage. We could go out in the middle of the week for an Italian meal, just because we fancied it. Heck, we went on a holiday to Disney.

All in all, 2007 was an astonishing year. Along with tours of Ireland, I took the show to Florida, Vermont, Malta, New York, Dubai and Adelaide. It was well received everywhere, even if it was not always completely sold out. I went to Florida two weeks after the Olympia and there were just a dozen people for my first matinee. I remember thinking, 'So, in just a fortnight I have gone from twelve hundred to twelve.' That sort of thing stops you being too pleased with yourself. It was a terrific year but I was not at home much and missed out on family life. My accountant asked me how long I was out of the country and when I totted it up I realised I had been abroad so much that I was tax exempt. In the autumn of that year, I also did a long UK tour so rarely slept in my own bed. One day, I got a plaintive reminder of how much my daughter Nancy was missing me.

She was looking at a poster for the show that's up on our office wall and suddenly wailed: 'I hate Tom Crean. Why can't my daddy work in Asda?' A seven-year old girl doesn't care that her parents now have a pension, their own home and security, she just wants to spend time with her dad. I comforted myself with the thought that she would, hopefully, thank me one day.

9
WE ARE ALL STORYTELLERS

Scott was always the class of officer that if he had something he knew you didn't want to hear, he couldn't look you in the eye to say it, he looked behind you or below you. Totally, totally different from Shackleton. Chalk and cheese, those two men. Now I am the only man to serve with both under real pressure, so I suppose I can say that. I am not saying they weren't great leaders both of them, but they were different. I would have gone with either to the last place on earth, they would just drag you in a different way.

From *Tom Crean – Antarctic Explorer* (Aidan Dooley)

What do Antarctic explorers talk about all day as they are trudging through the snow? This is what I asked a real-life explorer who had come to see the show. He looked quite amazed at my question. 'Nothing,' was his reply. 'The wind is so strong that you can't hear anything at all.' Instead of talking, he explained, you keep your head down and measure your steps – one, two, three, four – like a form of meditation. I remembered this little nugget, filed it away and eventually worked it into the script. Over the years, I have met many people who have informed and shaped the show. Be it an audience member, an explorer, a polar expert or someone who knew Tom, they have all given me authentic details, information or opinions that have enriched the play in some way. Whether I have added these details into the script or just let them fuel my imagination while performing, their contributions have been invaluable.

It has been a privilege and a pleasure to get to know Tom's family, his daughters and their children, and they have given me some indispensable insights into Tom the man. Not so much Tom the explorer, mind. As his daughters Eileen and Mary told me, their father rarely talked about his Antarctic adventures. He kept his medals – now in the Kerry County Museum in Tralee –

Mary (*left*) and Eileen Crean O'Brien with Aidan Dooley (*centre*) in 2002. Aidan performed an extract at the Midwinter Dinner, an annual fundraising celebration organised by The Tom Crean Society. He was costumed in a Royal Navy uniform of 1916 as Tom's daughters wanted to see their father portrayed in uniform and 'not all that dirty Antarctic stuff'.

hidden away in a box. I guess it's a bit like men who came home from the world wars: you just didn't want to share those harrowing stories. And, as Tom would have been only too aware, after the 1916 Rising, anyone who served with the British Army or the Royal Navy was considered a traitor to Ireland. But Mary and Eileen both gave me some

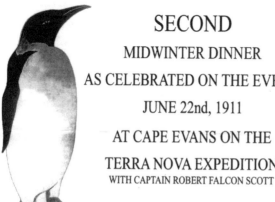

SECOND

MIDWINTER DINNER

AS CELEBRATED ON THE EVE OF

JUNE 22nd, 1911

AT CAPE EVANS ON THE

TERRA NOVA EXPEDITION
WITH CAPTAIN ROBERT FALCON SCOTT

DECEMBER 12TH, 2003

Special Guests

Mary & Eileen Crean O'Brien & Family

Broke Evans & family

Freddy Markham, Judy Skelton

Chris & Annie Wilson

Falcon & Jane Scott

Jonathan & Daphne Shackleton

An information card was given out at the Midwinter Dinner, listing the special guests, who were all descendants of expedition members.

lovely snippets about their father. Warmly gracious, they have been very supportive of the show from the moment they first saw it in Tralee during that weekend back in 2001. By that time they were both in their eighties and lived in Tralee. The two sisters had married brothers called O'Brien and lived next door to one another in houses called 'Discovery' and 'Terra Nova'. Isn't that fantastic? From Eileen and Mary, I discovered that Tom's feet were entirely black from frostbite and the only people to see them were the young children whom he used to meet down by the river during the days of his retirement in Annascaul. Taking off his socks and shoes, he would dangle his feet in the water as he told stories about the bottom of the world to his young audience – unlike his daughters, those children got to hear about his adventures as a polar explorer, perhaps a very edited version.

It was Eileen who told me about the time her father nearly lost a barrel of beer. Tom really had nothing to do with the running of the pub, the South Pole Inn. That was left to his wife, Nell, and also Eileen, who was the more practical of the two sisters. One weekend, Nell had gone away in her fur coat to a get-together of the Irish Country Women's Association in Dingle and daughter Eileen was pulling pints, as usual, when the barrel needed changing. Not strong enough to whack the peg in the cask herself, she asked her father to help. Unfortunately, Tom didn't really know what he was doing and lost half the barrel on the cellar floor, as it was spurted out all over the place. 'Don't tell your mother,' he implored Eileen. While Nell was a feisty woman by all accounts, Tom did not live in fear of her, as another anecdote revealed. One Friday morning, there were some men working on the roads outside the pub and Tom invited them inside for breakfast. Nell generally rose late after working nights in the bar, but the smell of frying bacon (strictly taboo for good Catholics on a Friday) brought her out of bed. She called down from the top of the stairs, 'Don't you know it's Friday?' Tom apparently called back to her, 'If you had been where I had been, you would know I'd eat the fat off your arse!' This was, I guess, Tom's way of saying that in the South Pole you would be thankful for any food on any day of the week.

While Tom faced unimaginable real dangers on his expeditions, he also saw plenty of dangers lurking in the sleepy village of Annascaul as far as his daughters were concerned. Eileen and Mary told me that when they went to the local hop on a Sunday night, Tom would insist on walking them the short distance up the road to the community hall. He would be there waiting for them when they came out, too. Perhaps all those years in the navy's male-only environments made him distrustful of men.

Also offering wonderful personal insights about Tom was his godson John Knightley. John's mother was Tom's cousin and his father was the railway stationmaster in Annascaul. John's father remembered Tom during his later years, walking to the station to pick up the *Daily Mail* newspaper, which arrived on the single-track trains that used to run rather randomly to the village. (The timetable was never adhered to as the twice-daily tides covered the rail in Blennerville – thus the train ran when it ran!) The paper was probably a few days out of date by the time Tom read it but it provided news about what was happening in the navy, which was clearly still of great interest to Tom after he retired. John also told me how much Tom loved children, so much so that if Tom ever came to visit the Knightleys at the children's bedtime and John's mother saw him walking up the path, she would lock the door to stop Tom getting in because he made the children too giddy with excitement.

Such stories revealed Tom the family man and were like precious little gems to me. I spent an afternoon with John, a wonderful man, who, like Eileen, has since died. Over tea and cake, John told me about how he used to go for a walk with his godfather every day after school. Tom would say to him, 'Be good at maths now and I'll get you into the navy.' One day, they were climbing the cliffs overlooking Inch beach, where the film *Ryan's Daughter* was shot. Tom's dog was chasing rabbits and he fell down a hole and was killed stone dead. Dog lover Tom, who always called his dogs Milo or Toby after the pups he'd been forced to shoot during the *Endurance* expedition, was distraught. In floods of tears, he made a hole on the beach and buried his dog. The following day, Tom turned up to meet John after school with a shovel and said, 'Now we are going to bury him properly.'

These insights into Tom are not in the show but they really enhanced my understanding and feeling for him and so informed my performance. Other stories were worked directly into the show, such as the fact that you can't afford to be caught napping in the South Pole. I learned this from a fascinating individual (whose name, alas, I cannot recall) with whom I worked at the Transport Museum and who built for me a touring version of the sledge, which broke down into pieces like a jigsaw for carrying in a suitcase when taking the show abroad. He told me about the time he had spent in Scandinavia during his national service in the 1950s. One night he had gone out for a few pints and was walking back to his billet when he became very tired, so he sat down and promptly fell into an alcohol-induced sleep. Luckily, a sense of self-preservation made him wake up after a few seconds and in that moment he realised that, had he slept for much longer he would most certainly have died of hypothermia. Once I heard that story, I wanted it to go in my show and I spent a while ruminating on how and where I would get it in. Finally, it became the line, 'If you fall asleep in the Antarctic, be God you fall asleep all right, because you never wake up.'

Another audience member, who had lived in the South Pole as part of a scientific study, told me a chilling story that once again demonstrated just how inhuman, how ferocious, how unforgiving, is the cold. This individual had decided to live on his own, away from everyone else in the main module and, to make sure that he would not lose his way in the event of a blizzard, there was a line staked in the snow from his module to the main door. Twelve years previously, another researcher had been staying in that same separate module and he struggled back to the main building in the middle of a really bad storm, a whiteout, in which he could see absolutely nothing. He got to the end of the staked-out line and knew that it ended three or four feet from the door, which opened outwards. At this point he tripped and fell over. When he got up, he didn't realise that, instead of now facing the door, he was facing the opposite way. He was completely disorientated in the whiteout. So as he moved forward, he was moving further away from the building and into a void. He was found three days later. They reckon that, in those temperatures, he would have been dead in an hour and a half. He had been inches from safety. That really brought home to me how fragile life is in Antarctica.

It was at the Shackleton School in Athy that I found another little nugget. In the question-and-answer session after the show, Shackleton's great-nephew Jonathan asked me, 'What would you have liked to ask Tom if you were to have met him?' I answered, 'I would have asked him why he went three times.' Jonathan's reply was, 'Ah, Aidan, you've never been.' An interesting answer, I thought at the time. But of course he had a point. The awe-inspiring majesty of the Antarctic will only reveal itself to you once you're there, as I was to discover for myself. So Jonathan's comment, 'You've never been!' was worked into the script.

Pat Falvey, who led an Irish team to the South Pole in 2007, was struck by the accuracy of the details in my show, such as what it is like to look down a mountain crevasse with the light bouncing around like a prism. But not everyone with insider knowledge thought I'd got it right. In 2003 I was invited by the Tom Crean Society to perform the show in Annascaul to celebrate a new statue of Tom that had been erected in a memorial garden opposite the South Pole Inn. The idea was that I would perform outside in the park with the statue in full view but, Ireland being Ireland, it started raining forty-five minutes or so into the performance. So we moved into the room above the pub and I carried on there. At the end of the show, there was a bit of a chat and Falcon Scott, grandson of Robert, stood up and said, 'I enjoyed your performance, Mr Dooley, but I have to say, here in front of everyone, that my grandfather would not have done something as stupid as that.' He was alluding to the part of the show when I make comparison between Scott and Shackleton as leaders of men. If you remember, my initial brief in creating the show had been to compare the leadership styles of the two men. I didn't really follow that brief once I got into telling Tom's story but I had written a paragraph that was a little nod towards it. I talked about how, on the one hand, Scott made his men slob the deck at 6 a.m. and how futile an exercise this was inside the Arctic Circle when the water would freeze and they would then

In full flow: Aidan Dooley performs in the memorial garden in Annascaul beside the newly unveiled statue of Tom Crean in 2003.

have to spend two hours chipping away at the ice. On the other hand, you had Shackleton, who turned back from the South Pole with just 97 miles to go because two of his men were sick, provisions were low and he did not want to risk everyone's lives. As a comparison, it was clearly weighted in favour of Shackleton, and Falcon Scott, understandably, took umbrage at the reference and the comparison I chose to make between Shackleton and his grandfather.

I remember clearly how I responded to Falcon Scott's objection. I said to him: 'I'm not a curatorial historian, but I guarantee you, sir, that I would not have put that in unless I'd read it somewhere.

But I will check and make sure of its accuracy and I will then consider whether or not it needs to be in. The last thing I would ever want to do is upset you or the families of any of these incredible men.' Afterwards, Brooke Evans, son of the Lieutentant Evans whose life Tom had saved so nobly, came up to me and said, 'That wasn't really cricket. He shouldn't have said that in front of everyone, he should have had a quiet word with you.' Brooke said he would endeavour to find out the truth about Scott having his men swab the deck and he would let me know. Three weeks later Brooke phoned me and said that he had got to the bottom of the reference. He discovered that Scott had set the men to work in order to help them avoid getting scurvy. At the time, no one knew of the link between a lack of vitamin C and scurvy, and medical opinion was that keeping active was the best way to avoid it. So Scott kept the men busy in what seemed a pointless exercise because he thought it would keep them healthy. An altruistic motive rather than a high-handed one. In the end, I took that original paragraph out of the show. I needed to prune the script anyway because the running time was getting longer, but also out of consideration for Scott's family. Why upset someone if you don't have to? So now I simply say that Scott and Shackleton were as different as chalk and cheese: 'I would have gone with either to the end of the earth, they would just drag you in a different way.' Job done.

It has been an interesting journey for me, this show, because it is so unlike any other piece of theatre I have ever been in. Normally, you have a director and writer to collaborate with and keep your performance on the straight and narrow. But I did not have any rehearsal time and no director. I just wrote it, put it in front of people at the museum and discovered what worked and what didn't. Basically, if it didn't hold people's attention, I would change my performance and the material until it did. I kept this same way of working once I put the show on the road and took it into theatres. I was forever checking in with the audience reaction, keeping an eye on any moments that worked well, or ceased to work well or, if I tried something new, that just didn't work at all. As producer, director, writer, actor, I have had to be rigorous, disciplined and very honest with myself. On stage I would always have half an eye on the effect I am having on the audience. I would come home from a performance and sometimes worry myself to death with what I had just done. Why had that bit not worked? Did they become a bit bored and restless in that section? Why were people not laughing at that bit any more? Should they be laughing at all?

Making people laugh is one of the highlights of our job. There is nothing more satisfying to an actor than hearing the rumble of an audience belly laugh (unless perhaps it's the silence of an audience moved to tears). I confess that, in common with a lot of actors, I will look for the laugh in any moment on stage and my instinct is to try, if at all possible, to have people in stitches. This is not altogether about an actor's ego; sometimes laughter is a true-to-life release from tragedy or sadness. Even so, it is fair to say I have struggled with the comedic elements in my play. Laughter shows you that an audience is engaged and entertained but, on the other hand, sometimes I wondered if I was being disrespectful to Tom's memory. This is a story of heroism, of death and courage and resilience in the face of adversity. Should people find this funny? Over the years, I have realised that laughter has a very welcome and respectful place in the show. While Tom and I are unlike in many ways, he shared with me the desire and ability to make people laugh and to brighten a dire situation with a quip or joke. His cheeriness, even his (apparently) awful singing cheered many a bleak moment down south. On stage, many people have found Tom very humorous, too. It's entirely up to me, the performer, to control when and why people laugh. If I become too clever with it, too deliberate, then Tom loses his modesty and humility, which I think were at the core of him. So I can't be too much of a smart alec because it wouldn't be true to the spirit of Tom.

Some audiences don't find me funny at all, in which case, I tighten up all the places where people usually laugh and just drive on through. Others find me raucously funny from the get-go and sometimes – this is very tricky – just one or two people may be amused. If I think the audience is laughing too much or inappropriately, I will try to minimise it. Comedy is very technical, so if you can make a laugh you can break it too, by simply changing an inflection or taking out a pause. But who am I to say that the audience shouldn't laugh if they find something funny? All I can do is not chase laughs, which is sometimes quite hard for me. The only bad review I have read about my show was written by a journalist in Boston who criticised me heavily for being too funny, which he did not think was appropriate for the subject matter. In my defence, I have to say that on the opening night in Boston, the audience was almost entirely Irish or of Irish descent, so they understood and revelled in every Irish reference. Perhaps I was seduced by their laughter and I played up to it a wee bit. Maybe … but sometimes you just have to go with the flow. In any case, if you become too indulgent the audience will let you know because they won't find you funny any more. Some people I spoke to after the show said they were not expecting it to be funny and that they found they laughter a welcome relief, a great contrast, from some of the darker moments.

I see the play as a work in progress, even now. I have chucked out bits that did not work, added bits that I hoped would make it better. Apart from the facts of the story, the play never stays exactly the same: I am always trying to keep it fresh, make it sharper, funnier, more moving and – increasingly – shorter. I have always been aware of its running time and have never wanted it to get too long. As I have got older, so my energy on stage has slowed down. In some ways this suits the character of Tom better because he was slower and weightier than me. But now that I am a bit (okay, a lot) older, I have settled into a slower, more relaxed rhythm, I have had to trim down the script and this has meant losing some wonderful stories. There was the one when Shackleton saved a man's life by lifting him out of the water in his reindeer sleeping bag and instead of being grateful that he was still alive, the saved sailor was merely upset that he had lost his tobacco. Then there was the story about the men of the *Endurance*, adrift on the ice, getting very upset about the cry of the penguins because they thought it was a portent signifying imminent death – Tom dealt with the situation by taking a gun and shooting said penguins. These are tales that reveal the men in their humanity and it was hard to lose them, but the play was too long. I never want to outstay my welcome on stage and something had to go. I would get rid of the sections that didn't serve the main thrust of the story and move it forwards. I think writing teachers will tell you it's called 'killing your darlings'. Tough love.

There was another element of the show that I decided to lose once I went on tour. In the early days I would greet the audience as they came into the theatre and would chat to them as Tom. It was another way of breaking down the fourth wall, a technique I used a lot in museum work and there was no reason why it wouldn't work in theatres, too. Then one day I was doing a one-off performance at the National Portrait Gallery in Trafalgar Square, where there is a portrait of Scott. I was doing the show in a little lecture theatre in the basement of the gallery for people who regularly attended talks there. Before the show I approached some audience members who had arrived early, intending to chat to them in character as Tom and hopefully start to create an atmosphere for the story to come. But these lecture goers really didn't want to be talking to this strangely dressed, slightly scuzzy fella with the accent they couldn't understand, they just wanted to be left in peace to read their newspapers. They had no idea I was in the show and they were quite rude to me. So I started off the performance that day in a very bad mood. Eventually, in order to prevent the show being affected by how nice people were to me beforehand, I decided to stop the pre-show chat and start the play in a more theatrical way, which worked much better.

It has all been a process of trial and error, of discovering what works and what doesn't. As I have changed, become older and more relaxed, so has the play. However, some things remain constant, including the pacing of the first and second half. The first half is more leisurely, chattier, if you like. Once I got into theatres, as opposed to noisy museums, it became possible to slow down the pace even more at some points and have moments of total silence or stillness on stage. These moments have been a revelation to me – it's wonderful to suspend time on stage and for just a few seconds for actor and audience to hold their collective breath. One of those moments is when Shackleton staggers into the whaling station at Stromness after crossing South Georgia and summoning all that is left of his strength, manages to spit out the words to the amazed Norwegian in front of him: 'I … AM … SHACKLETON'. With those three words I try to convey something of the pain, the exhaustion, the determination, the sheer superhuman effort that has just been summoned by these men to complete their astonishing journey. An audience member once asked me, 'How do you know those whalers spoke English?' A good point. I didn't know for sure but, I reasoned, it was a good chance they did. And even if they didn't, I think they would have understood his name, they would have got the gist that this broken, snow-ravaged, filthy, hairy man in front of them was none other than Ernest Shackleton.

The second half of the show is deliberately much faster as a contrast to the first. I never want to let the pace drop: the audience should have no time to think, but just be swept along with the story and be consumed by it. I hardly draw breath in the telling of it and sometimes I have felt as though the audience stand at the end to acknowledge my sweaty expense of energy as much as anything else. Nowadays I have to dig deep to summon that kind of energy but summon it I must or the show won't work nearly as well. That's my belief anyway. I'm too fearful of tampering with the pace of the second half and so don't. The only time I have performed it at less than breakneck speed was out of necessity rather than choice (more of that in the next chapter). I have been aware more recently that the second half has become perhaps a little too flabby and therefore not quite as good. I wondered if this was why I wasn't getting as many standing ovations as I used to when I toured Ireland. So during my most recent tour, I trimmed down the script and picked up the pace so it was shorter and faster. The ovations returned, which just goes to prove that there can be nothing leisurely about that second half.

Doing the show has been a voyage of discovery for me and still is. Each show is a whole new story, with a different chemistry between me and the audience, a different energy, and that is what is so wonderful about doing live theatre. As I have said before (but I don't think you can say it too often), the real star of the show is Tom and his real-life story. I have always felt that it is my job to tell this story in the best way possible. Yes, I want to entertain people. I want to make them laugh and cry, and to immerse them in the world of the Antarctic. But most of all I want the audience to shake their head in disbelief that a human being could withstand such hardship, display so much courage and, most important of all, survive. If they understand that, then I will have done my job.

10
ON THE ROAD

But then another voice started creeping in my ear and I tried not to listen I promise you, but in the end it was a very good-looking voice and she were saying, 'Sleep Tom, sleep Tom, come on …' Oh and I would have gladly! But for those that may not know, if you sleep in the Antarctic you never wake up. But it wasn't just me, was it? There were two men depending on me and that drives you on. And when we crossed the south Atlantic in the 23ft open boat there were twenty-two men depending on us. And as we crossed the unchartered glaciers of South Georgia there was twenty-five men depending on us. And that's what drives you on. Cherry-Garrard wrote in his diary: 'To die is the easy thing, to struggle to live is what true heroism is all about' and, I, Tom Crean, was struggling, struggling to live.

From *Tom Crean – Antarctic Explorer* (Aidan Dooley)

I remember one particular night when I had just performed a sell-out show in an atmospheric theatre converted from an old cinema. At the end, all 450 people stood and gave me a rapturous ovation. You might think that afterwards I would be revelling in praise from my many admirers over a pint or two of Guinness. You could be forgiven for thinking that this is how my evening unfolded, but you would be wrong. When I was on tour in the early days I would be lucky to meet even a single member of the audience once the show had come down because there was often still a lot of work for me to do. No sooner had I (and Tom) taken a bow than I was packing away the set and driving off to my B&B, which would vary in quality and comfort. On this particular night I was packing up in a deserted theatre. All the staff had gone apart from the fire officer who was hovering, clearly keen to get away and enjoy what was left of his night. Eventually he said, 'Look, I'll be off, just close the door behind you when you leave.' So I did. I finished packing, closed the door and drove back to the B&B. But after the euphoria of the performance, I just couldn't face the thought of the dreary little room on my own and did the only thing that could possibly have cheered me up: went off in search of a curry chip. I sat eating them in the car and made my nightly phone call to Miriam. I said to her: 'The show was great, everyone loved it. Now here I am, in my Ford Mondeo, having been abandoned by the theatre, eating a curry chip and going back to a B&B that doesn't even have a telly. Oh the glamour!'

Loneliness was the hardest thing for me about being on tour. A naturally gregarious soul, I don't do too well on my own and I really missed Miriam and the children. For the first eight years of touring Ireland I was a one-man band and did everything myself: that's all the driving, the get-ins and get-outs at venues, sorting out the lighting and sound with the theatre technician, organising props and costume, dressing the set. To be honest, it was a slog. I was doing everything a stage manager would do as well as performing a two-hour show. Having driven to the venue, sometimes over a long distance, I would probably have to be in the theatre from about 2.30 p.m. I might get an hour or two off for something to eat and a rest before it was on with the show. By the time I stepped out into the lights as Tom I had already done nearly a full day's work. And after the show, I didn't want to be a Nobby No Mates on my own in a pub so that people who had seen the show felt they had to come and talk to me. Usually, I would just go straight back to my digs: not exactly the most convivial end to what had been quite a solitary day. Finally, I employed a stage manager to travel with me, which meant I could keep some energy in reserve for the show itself. Just as important, it was also some company for me. I gently let it be known to the stage manager that eating the B&B breakfast with me was part of the job!

In spite of the slog and the hard work, touring is fantastically good fun. I have met some wonderful people, travelled to places I would never have been if it weren't for Tom and had some great adventures.

The eight weeks I spent in New York, performing at the Irish Rep theatre, were colourful and sometimes dramatic for the wrong reasons. I once had to stop the show because two women were on the point of a brawl because one had been kicking the back of the other's seat. While an Irish or English person might show their displeasure by huffing and puffing or tutting rather loudly, the American response was to shout out, 'Don't start, bitch!' I had a word with the women and made a joke of it, but they were not smiling. I could only hope that they did not start up again as I didn't fancy my chances of stopping a full-on fight. Luckily, peace reigned.

It was also in New York that I went on stage feeling so ill that I wasn't sure whether words or something else was going to come out of my mouth. I had started to feel ill about an hour before the show – sweaty and nauseous and altogether terrible. Normally when actors feel ill before a performance, we know that once we get on stage and the adrenaline kicks in, we will, in all likelihood, be absolutely fine. But this was different and I knew that Dr Theatre would not be able to sort it out. I summoned the stage manager and said I didn't feel at all well. She took one look at me and instead of making reassuring noises she just said, 'Oh Jesus.' That's when I knew I was in serious trouble. The woman who ran the theatre, Charlotte, a former nurse, told me to take some flat coke on stage and sip it when I felt sick, which I did. She instructed a young lad working at the theatre to stand by in the wings with a bucket. Charlotte also said that I didn't have to go on and that they could cancel the show, but I wanted to take my chances. It was a Thursday night and I was due home on the Monday after eight weeks away. I was very keen not to cancel the show in case I was obliged to do another one that interfered with my going home.

How I got through that performance I will never know. On stage I was desperately working out which bits I could cut. I staggered through the first half having slashed it by over twenty minutes. At the interval, I sat crying backstage, without even the strength to get to the dressing room. I was so hot that I stripped off all my clothes and just sat there sobbing. That poor young intern who was backstage with me – the one in charge of the bucket – was wearing a tortured expression and did not know where to look. I somehow made it through the whole show without throwing up or fainting. I had no pace and no energy; I was speaking very slowly, taking a breath between each line in order not to be sick. It is a pace that, ordinarily, I would have imagined would kill the show stone dead. But for some reason, it worked. Perhaps it was because I wasn't pushing too hard. It astounded me that no one watching the play had any idea of the onstage struggle I was having just to stay upright. I received a fantastic response from the audience. The next day, I met an American actor who was rehearsing in the building and had come to see the show the night before. He was wildly enthusiastic. 'It was magnificent, like a masterclass in acting,' he said. 'And that breathing between the lines – that was extraordinary.'

It was no surprise that a lot of Irish Americans came to see the show during that New York run and they were fantastically positive audiences. But after a couple of weeks people stopped finding me funny and there was no longer any audible response to anything I was doing. I started to think I'd lost it and so I asked Ciaran, the guy who ran the theatre, to come and see the show. Over a drink afterwards I asked him, 'So what's going wrong? Why don't people find it funny any more?' Ciaran explained that nothing was going wrong and that it was just a different type of audience. Once all the Irish diaspora had been to see it, what was left in New York in August was the regular, solid theatre-going audience who were mostly Jewish. 'They are there to have a cultural experience and don't know the difference between Kerry and Cork,' he told me. 'But they are really enjoying it, just very quietly.' Once I understood this, I felt relieved of the responsibility of being funny. I did, however, add in another joke during that time, one that did not rely on a knowledge of Ireland or the Irish. Like most of the humour in the play, it was a moment that came out of a spontaneous ad-lib during performance. I don't know why I thought it up or where it came from, but it was in the bit when Crean manages to reach Hut Point to rescue Lieutenant Evans and Bill Lashly. 'They went to the officers' side of the hut and brought back a bottle of brandy, the quality of which was so high it was walking in on its own,' was what I said. For once, the New York theatre set was amused, so the joke stayed in.

I have been endlessly fascinated by the different cultural reactions to the play around the world. In Northern Ireland, for example, people were really not amused by the jibes Tom makes about the British Army, whereas British audiences enjoyed them enormously. In Northern Ireland, they were not getting that it was a navy fella making jokes about an army fella, or a working-class seaman making jokes about the posh officer class. I felt that they were hearing an Irish republican taking a pot shot at the British Army. One of the guaranteed laugh lines in the show is when Tom says, 'That young officer turns round to me and Bill and says something I only heard once in twenty-seven years in the Royal Navy. A British officer said, "I've made a mistake". Can you believe that?' When that was met with silence – not even a titter – during my first performance in the North, I knew what to expect. It was slightly different in Derry, where the audience was predominantly nationalist and I would sell out the show. In Belfast, I was getting small audiences of around forty-five and after the show I said to one woman, 'Although we are on the same piece of land, it's like a different country here, isn't it?' This woman who was, shall we say, of a certain ilk, said, 'Well yes, of course it is, because we *are* a different country.' I felt that it was a bit too soon for the North to be laughing at itself.

The fact that the show is enjoyed in different cultures is, I think, something to do with the fact that it's a simple piece of storytelling and the story itself is a cracker. Someone asked me where it wouldn't work and I said anywhere that English is not the first language, or to be more precise, where the audience are not English speakers. Most audiences, even in places such as Dubai, were predominantly English or Irish ex-pats. Not, however, in Buenos Aires. I performed it there at a cultural event for the Irish Embassy. Most of the audience were Argentinians who didn't understand English, or at least not at the pace I was delivering it and they just did not have a clue what was going on. I had to stop the show twice because they kept standing up to take photographs. I was going mad. At the interval, the Irish ambassador had to have a little chat with them about the cultural differences between us and how in our country it is not considered good manners to take photos or indeed answer your mobile phone during a performance.

Mobile phones are, in fact, a curse wherever I perform. Because I talk directly to the audience, I can't help seeing the telltale light of someone texting when I look out into the darkness of the auditorium. It is really distracting. I usually stare at the culprit for a bit and give them ten seconds' grace before

I say something to draw attention to the sneaky texter. Food can also be a showstopper and not in a good way. I once halted the show because there appeared to be a group halfway back in the stalls who were merrily eating their lunch along with all the sound effects of bags and bottles being opened. It was as if a group of scouts was having a picnic. I honestly think they were surprised that it would bother anyone. It sounds as if I am always stopping the show to berate an audience but I really have not had to do it very often and I try not to, partly because it would alienate the audience by coming across as a precious thespian and also because it stops the flow of the show and sometimes makes me forget what comes next. It's not unknown for me to have to ask the audience what I was saying before I was interrupted. I have sometimes stopped it for the fun, such as the time a man had to answer the call of nature. Because of the layout of the studio, he had to pass in front of the whole audience – and me – on his way out. I paused and looked at him and he realised all eyes were on him. 'I'll be back,' says yer man. 'Well, don't flush because we can hear it,' was my retort. The poor man scuttled out to peals of good-natured laughter.

By far my most spectacular case of amnesia was nothing to do with a mobile phone or cheese butties.

It was during what was probably my fourth run at the Civic Theatre in Tallaght. I was on stage, tootling along nicely and was about fifteen minutes into the show when I opened my mouth to speak but I didn't know what to say. My mind had gone totally blank and I had no notion of what came next, and I mean none: nada, zilch. I couldn't even tell you where I was in the play, so I couldn't jump to the next bit that I did know. By this time I had been doing the show for a good eight years and I knew it inside out. But on this night, my mind was totally and utterly blank. It was the strangest and most horrible sensation – the actor's dreaded 'dry'. When I look back at why it happened I realise it was because I had added in a new line when I had last performed it. That had been about six months earlier so there had been no time to run it in or make it familiar like the rest of my lines. This new line had thrown my whole memory out of whack. That's what I understood only afterwards, which was a comfort because otherwise I might have thought that it was old age or me losing my capacity to remember.

But at the time it was happening I had no notion of this, I was just blank. On stage. With 300 people looking at me. What to do? Don't panic, I kept telling myself. Don't tell the audience either. My first instinct might have been to share the state of affairs with the audience and get them to help me out but some instinct told me not to. Those poor people had paid twenty euro or so to see me and I couldn't tell them, fifteen minutes into the show, that I didn't know what the hell came next. There wasn't even a script that I could run and get from my dressing room. After a while, which felt like years but was probably a few seconds, I thought I had better break the silence and say something. So I looked at the audience and said, 'It was very cold, you know.' Then, think Aidan think. Say something else. 'Yes, the sort of cold that would kill you.' I sat down. 'Yes, awful cold.' I walked around. Still nothing, so I decided to talk about the *Discovery*, as it was Tom's first ship south, and as I did, I suddenly remembered a line, a point in the script that I could go to and from that marvellous stepping stone I was back on track. After the show, a man asked me to sign his programme. He said he'd seen the show four times. I told him, 'You've seen something different tonight,' and he said, 'Ah yes.' I don't know if that was him acknowledging my dry and I couldn't bring myself to confess to it because it was still too raw. That sort of hiccough could put fear in you that it would happen again and that way stage fright lies. But luckily, I realised why I had gone blank. It was that pesky new line. I went over and over that section before the next show and locked it into my memory. It never happened again.

It always amazes and comforts me when things go wrong on stage and the audience think it's supposed to happen, or just don't notice. British Airways once lost my costume when I flew over to Dublin to perform at the Olympia. The Abbey Theatre kindly helped me out and gave me a turn-of-the-century costume of a woollen jacket and trousers – what I called 'the *Playboy of the Western World* outfit'. I didn't have the Burberry or all the essential bits of the costume that I talk about at the top of the show, so I just described them to the audience instead of showing them. When I came offstage at the interval, there was my recovered lost bag sitting there. Too late for that night – I could hardly revert to my usual costume halfway through, though I was sorely tempted as those borrowed woollen trousers made me even hotter and sweatier than usual. Afterwards I was chatting to Aonghus McAnally, son of the late, great Irish actor Ray. Aonghus was the producer of the RTÉ radio programme that had given me such good publicity for the show during my first time at Andrews Lane Theatre. He had seen my play at least once and maybe twice before. When we chatted after the show and I told him what had happened – because I guessed he would be wondering why

Tom was in such a strange get-up – Aonghus had not even noticed that I was minus the Burberry and wearing a completely different costume. Something that had seemed so crucial to me turned out to be not so crucial after all …

I have returned to the Olympia many times now and the doorman always greets me like an old friend. I am delighted and surprised that the show can still attract a healthy audience there. It is not selling out like it did in the earlier years but there are still plenty of people who want to see it. It always feels good to be back in Ireland, to bring the show home. It has been fantastic to spread the word about Tom to other countries, but artistically and for the fun, the craic, I like playing in Ireland best. Without being aware of it, I think I have written for an Irish audience: maybe not in the first instance when I wrote it for the museum, but certainly over the years as I have adapted, refined and hopefully improved it. Not only do the Irish get the humour, but I don't have to tone down the accent or slow down the pace like I do in other countries. I think the show feels at its most authentic in Ireland.

Wherever I perform the show, it seems to hold up well. In places such as Finland and Norway, they really understand the nature of the Arctic cold and how it can kill you in a heartbeat, so they really appreciated the heroism of those lionhearted men. In New Zealand, people connected with the story because so many of those Antarctic expeditions had begun and ended there. The punishing cold did not strike quite the same chord in the sunshine of Florida, where my first audience totalled a dozen people. It was very strange indeed to be talking about the perishing cold in the blazing Florida heat and it was very rare for there to be anyone in the audience without a blue rinse and an OAP pass. But audiences steadily grew and by the second week it was a sunny sell-out.

Being in the appropriate environment does not, on the other hand, always guarantee a good night, as I discovered not so long ago when I returned to Norway. The performance was in Oslo in a museum built around the *Fram*, the ship that Amundsen and all the Norwegian explorers had used over a century ago. So it was a brilliantly atmospheric venue. Trouble was, I was the St Patrick's Day entertainment and was trying to do a truncated twenty-minute version of the show to people who were more interested in sipping champagne, eating canapés and chatting than listening to a word I said. It was a pretty horrendous experience. However, the next night, some local artists had arranged for me to do the show in a lovely little theatre some twenty minutes outside Oslo. That turned out to be a great night, packed with Irish and Norwegians who really got it. It made the trip to Oslo really worthwhile.

As I have toured with Tom, I try to make myself at home, albeit very briefly, in each new venue. To that end, I carry around with me a box of tricks containing cherished photos, pictures, letters and gifts that I have collected along this marvellous journey with Mr Crean. The first thing I do when I get to a new dressing room is to put out my laminated photos of Tom, one with him smoking his pipe, one with his beloved pups and the one in which he is carrying skis. I also put out family pictures that have accompanied me since I first started touring, photos of Liam aged eight, Nancy at about two or three, as well as pictures of Miriam and my parents. I also put up a good luck card that Nancy gave me about ten years ago. Then out comes my scruffy little blue towel, on which I lay out my make-up. Nowadays, as I am trying to fight the effects of age and stay as healthy as possible, I also have multivitamins laid out along with everything else.

Like many actors I am a little bit superstitious before a performance and have my little rituals that I never want to vary in case it brings bad luck. I like to get to the theatre about an hour and a half

Aidan's dressing room with photos of Tom Crean and of Aidan's family on the mirror. He brings these photos with him wherever he performs.

before curtain up and I check props and the stage setting. Since I've had sciatica trouble with my back, I always try to lie down in the dressing room for a while and do the Alexander technique exercises. In case I drop off, which is always a possibility, I ask the stage manager to come and wake me at the half (thirty-five minutes before curtain up). I always play the same piece of music before the show, which is Dido's album *Life for Rent*. Then I put on my costume in the same sequence before slapping on a bit of make-up, some brown on my face to give the impression of a tan and dirt on my hands and under my nails. For about two hours before a show I drink only water, never a hot drink, to protect my voice. Then before I leave the dressing room I always touch Tom's picture, the one with the pipe, and ask him to be with me. I like to be at the side of the stage for a few minutes and listen to the buzz of the audience. Then I remind myself that I must perform the show as if for the first time and on I go. It would be all too easy to get into a well-oiled, automatic rhythm on stage after performing the show hundreds of times, but I try to keep it as fresh and surprising as I can.

Sometimes, it's me that's surprised when people offer up a bit of audience participation. Recently, for example, I was doing the show in Thurles in County

Aidan clears his head before getting started with the prep routine he carries out before each performance.

Tipperary and came to the point when Tom thinks mistakenly that the dying Lieutenant Evans has finally succumbed to scurvy and breathed his last. I said the line, 'He suddenly stopped and crumpled to the ice. There was no movement out of him. He was dead.' And in the dramatic pause that I left afterwards, a little voice piped up, 'No, he isn't!' It was a young boy in the audience who clearly knew the story and had become so engrossed that he felt he ought to let Tom know that Evans was alive after all. It was wonderfully funny and touching. But I had to think quickly as to how I should deal with it, because I wanted to keep going yet I didn't want to ignore him. So I said, 'Just let me get to the end, young man.' I carried on until I got to the line, 'He wasn't dead at all,' which I delivered in the direction of the boy. At this, the whole audience erupted into laughter and spontaneous applause. It was a marvellous moment. There was another slightly less gratifying, though equally funny, moment at the end of another show. When Tom imagines what it would be like to be the first Irishman to see the South Pole, I used to ask the audience. 'Wouldn't it be magnificent?' Out of the darkness came the reply, 'No, not really.' I stopped asking the question after that.

One of the joys of being on the road with Tom has been meeting the people who come to see it. Now that I have a stage manager and don't do quite so many one-night stands, I am not quite the solitary hermit I once was. In Ireland I have returned to the same venues many times and it has been great to see familiar faces coming back again to see it, or to be welcomed by theatre staff who now know me. I have been lucky enough to make a few good friends along the way, including Paul and Neasa Callaghan from Cork. I first met Paul after he had come to see the show and was telling him how lonely I found it on the road. He immediately said, 'Next time you

Aidan packs everything into his trusty car boot during one of his tours.

are in Cork, you must stay with us.' I have enjoyed their hospitality on many occasions and they became firm friends with Miriam and me. It was Paul who accompanied me on my unforgettable trip to the Antarctic (see next chapter). I will be eternally grateful to Eileen Sheridan and John Morgan, my generous, gracious friends who have welcomed me into their homes during the weeks I have performed in Dublin and saved me from many a lonely night. I have also made a fine friend in Dave McGilton, a very talented musician whom I met after he got in touch to say he had been inspired by the show to write some music for it. I loved what he wrote and said I would find a way to work it into the play if possible. Eventually I found just the right spot and it became the stirring verse that Tom sings just after he and Shackleton have rescued all twenty-two men from Elephant Island:

Eyes to the west boys, take her out slow.
Back to the wind, forty below.
Hands to the wheel boys, keep her in line.
Send down the word, we're going home.

Among my audiences there has occasionally been a famous face or two and I have managed to meet them with my trousers on (remember GayByrnegate?). As well as actor Milo O'Shea and *Angela's Ashes* author Frank McCourt, I have also met and enjoyed dinner with film director David Puttnam. I was chatting with actor Jeremy Irons after he had come to see the show in Gougane Barra, in west Cork and he invited me to visit his castle in west Cork. We had a lovely three hours when, cheroot in hand, Jeremy showed me around his beautiful home, including the jacuzzi on the roof with its views of Cape Clear island.

I met Princess Anne after she came to see the show in Dundee, at the museum built around Scott's ship, *Discovery*. Princess Anne is patron of the South Georgia Trust and I was performing the show as part of an effort to help rid the island of rats. Like the elk, which were brought to South Georgia by Norwegian whalers, rats are not indigenous to the island and were disturbing the ecology of South Georgia, especially in relation to the penguin colonies. My show was part of a fundraising event that would hopefully kick-start the rat-eradication programme. I was originally going to do the full show cut down to an hour and a half, but in the end I did only the first half, so ironically I did not get to tell the tale of Shackleton and his historic crossing of South Georgia. Nevertheless, it went down a storm. Performing in front of the Princess Royal gave an extra weight to the moment when I describe Tom receiving his Albert Medal from the King – Princess Anne's own great-grandfather, George V.

One is not allowed to keep the Princess Royal waiting afterwards so there was no time for a wash or change after the performance – I must have been a sorry, sweaty sight as I chatted away to her. The first thing she asked me was, 'Do you do this as your main job?' I wasn't offended. She also asked me why Tom Crean had been such an unknown figure in Ireland and I found myself talking about the Ireland that Tom came back to. So there I was, discussing with the Queen's only daughter the plight of the Irishmen who fought for British King and country in the First World War and were treated like traitors by the new Ireland. Instead of saying, 'Really? Gosh, I didn't know that,' the Princess had a way of saying, 'Yes,' with an inflection that suggested she already knew all about it. However, we had an interesting chat for about twenty minutes and she asked me all about Shackleton and his extraordinary journey. I felt that she had genuinely engaged with the show and its content. Her equerry told me that he had not heard her laugh so much during a show for years. I felt rather pleased about that. I guess her family's connection with the navy and armed forces helped her connect with the humour. Before I went on stage that day, I had touched Tom's picture as usual and said to him, 'Tom, I am going to tell your story now to the daughter of the Queen of England. How far have you come, boyo?' But then, Tom had already done the Royal thing a century earlier – and he had the medals to prove it. I think we can safely say that Tom Crean had come much further than most people could ever dream of. In my slightly less heroic world, meanwhile, I still felt a certain satisfaction that a princess had laughed at my jokes.

Through Tom I also went to Buckingham Palace to meet Queen Elizabeth II in 2012, as part of an event honouring our renowned explorers. When the invitation arrived in the post, I was on tour and when Miriam read the envelope, which had a royal crest and said, 'From the Master of the House' she thought it was some sort of clever new mail scam. It was an unforgettable day at the palace. Standing alongside author Michael Smith, I was lined up with climbing legends Ranulph Fiennes and Chris Bonnington, along with celebrities such as David Walliams and Ben Fogle. As the Queen approached, Michael and I exchanged glances. Both non-royalist, socialist lefties at heart, we were not sure what to do in terms of etiquette. But actually the Queen is so small that you can't help but drop down to shake her hand, so it didn't feel compromising to lower

The Master of the Household
has received Her Majesty's command to invite

Mr. Aidan Dooley

to a Reception to be given at Buckingham Palace by
The Queen and The Duke of Edinburgh
for those involved in Exploration and Adventure
on Thursday, 8th December, 2011 at 6.00 p.m.

A reply is requested to:
The Master of the Household
Buckingham Palace
London SW1A 1AA   *Dress: Lounge Suit / Day Dress*
Email: master.household@royal.gsx.gov.uk

Guests are asked to arrive between 5.30 and 5.50 p.m.

Aidan's invitation to Buckingham Palace in 2011 and his name tag for the event.

MR. AIDAN DOOLEY

THEATRE ACTOR

my head. The Duke of Edinburgh asked me, 'So are you an explorer?' and I replied, 'No, just pretending to be one.' We both chuckled. It was a huge moment for me in terms of Tom being recognised. Here I was, in the Throne Room of Buckingham Palace, chatting to explorers and celebrities, walking the red-carpeted halls, all because of Tom. It was a privilege to be remembering all those great men who had been so heroic and I felt the same way when, later that year, I was invited to St Paul's Cathedral to mark the centenary anniversary of Captain Scott's ill-fated expedition. I am glad to be able to play a part in keeping alive the memory of one of those extraordinary explorers. Tom Crean is no longer unsung or forgotten but takes his rightful place as hero and respected member of the Golden Age of Exploration. And to prove it, there I was, chomping on canapés at Buckingham Palace.

11
THE BOTTOM OF THE EARTH

Ssh ... isn't silence lovely? ... Sometimes when the wind drops you can hear the Antarctic silence.

From *Tom Crean – Antarctic Explorer* (Aidan Dooley)

It was 6 a.m. and I was on the deck of a Russian icebreaker, taking in my first-ever glimpse of South Georgia in the southern Atlantic Ocean. It's over 1,200 miles from Ushuaia, at the southernmost end of South America, and more than 800 miles from Elephant Island. Over the previous decade, as I had been recounting the stories of those heroic Edwardian explorers, the island had become an almost mythical place for me. Now here it was, coming into view in all its fearsome majesty. It is hard to explain just how jaw-droppingly awe-inspiring, how forbidding and how starkly beautiful was this landscape. As the ship nosed steadily through the waters of the Southern Ocean, it was absolutely incredible to watch these immense black rocks, those gigantic mountains rising graciously in front of my eyes. I could only marvel at how any man could measure themselves against them, as Tom Crean, Ernest Shackleton and Frank Worsley had done a century before when they became the first men ever to cross South Georgia's serrated spine.

It was through my friend Paul Callaghan that I finally got the opportunity to visit the Antarctic. Paul's friend Peter knew the Canadian owner of a ship called the *Polar Star*, a former Russian icebreaker that was taking a group of ornithologists and sightseers on an extensive tour of the Antarctic in December 2010. When Peter suggested that Tom Crean should be part of the trip, the owner was very positive and agreed to give me a very reduced fare to come along. I couldn't say no to such a wonderful opportunity, especially since Paul would be coming with me, meaning there was someone to share the whole experience with. I was beyond excited as we set off on the first leg of the journey, taking a British Airways flight from Heathrow to Buenos

Aires. At last I was going to see at first hand all the places that I had, thus far, been able to see only in my imagination. At Buenos Aires we took a smaller plane to Ushuaia, the Argentinian port from which the *Polar Star* would depart. We decided to get there in plenty of time because the boat would not wait if you weren't there: it was sailing at 4 p.m. on the Thursday, with or without Tom Crean and pals. The most southerly town in the world, Ushuaia really felt like frontier territory. With its brightly coloured houses of galvanised steel, and a backdrop of snow-capped mountains, it is the closest point of civilisation to the South Pole.

Oh and here's a tip for anyone thinking of taking a trip to the Antarctic (do it if you possibly can): make your own way to Ushuaia and then cut out the middleman by buying your Antarctic cruise ticket on the quayside there. It's half the price you'd pay to a travel company. We spent two days in Ushuaia. Our acclimatisation to the southern hemisphere included visiting grill rooms where people sliced chunks from whole sides of roasting cows and slapped down a plateful in front of you. It was here that I was also introduced to the nocturnal rumblings with which Paul serenaded me. Yes, he is quite the snorer and I was going to be sharing a ship's berth with him for three weeks. I couldn't

Percy penguin in Ushuaia during Aidan's trip to the Antarctic in December 2010.

even block it out with earplugs because my ears seem to be a funny shape and plugs never stay in (I know now I need wax ones). There was nothing for it but to drink sufficient alcohol before bedtime – at least that was my excuse.

Luckily, that was the only downside to travelling with Paul, who is enormously good company and great fun. He had brought with him a toy penguin that (ironically) snored when you pressed it. We had decided he was going to be our trip mascot and so over the course of the three weeks Percy penguin appeared in all our photos and videos. He was duly snapped walking up the steps to the ship as we boarded the *Polar Star*. The ship was not your Disney, all-singing, all-dancing, jacuzzi-on-the-upper-deck type of vessel that cruises out of Orlando or Miami. Originally a Russian naval ship, it was not designed as a pleasure boat but as a working ship that was able to break up ice in Arctic regions. It was bought by a Canadian company back in the 1990s and adapted into a polar cruise ship, but it still retained that Soviet feel, with its water pipes visible, for example. Luxurious it may not have been, but it was certainly very comfortable and – most importantly – there was nothing utilitarian about the food, which was absolutely delicious. Paul and I were sharing a small cabin that had a little window and wardrobe, and was so small that we could touch one another's bed from our own (or pinch a snorer's nose).

I am a terrible sailor. However, luckily, the previous summer I had met a woman in America who tipped me off about a device that you put on your arm that sends out electric impulses that sort of instruct your stomach not to be sick. It proved a godsend for me: I put it on whenever the sea was choppy and, with one notable exception, I did not

Paul Callaghan and Aidan, with Percy penguin, on the quayside in Ushuaia, in front of the former Russian icebreaker, *Polar Star*.

get sick. At the beginning of the voyage, one of the sailors was talking to us about boat etiquette and what to expect on the trip. He explained that because the ship was designed to bash through ice it didn't have a keel but instead had a tank in the bottom, which meant that it rocked a lot. As well as rocking backwards and forwards, he said, the ship would sometimes pitch from side to side. Now some people get sick when it rocks and others when it pitches, he told us, but everyone gets sick when it rocks, rolls and pitches! That only happened once, in a force 10 gale, and even my trusted bracelet couldn't help my bewildered stomach.

Our first stop was the Falkland Islands, which we reached after only a couple of days. We spent a day and a half there, going to see an albatross and penguin colony (the first of many on our trip). One of the islands we went to is about the size of Wales and it is so windswept that there are no trees. I took some footage with a camcorder and you can't hear a word because voices were just being blasted out by the ferocious winds. It was as we walked around the colonies and then later around Port Stanley that I started to chat to some of the other people on our voyage. Most of them were ornithologists, many Canadian, though there were a few Brits, and others, too. Paul and I were the only Irish on board, which made us feel a little bit special. There were some passengers we did not see during the entire trip because travel sickness confined them to their cabins. This included one poor Malaysian woman on her honeymoon (yes, of all the honeymoons they could have had, they chose to spend good money travelling in a rocking ship with a bunch of birdwatchers). In Port Stanley we saw a lot of people driving around in very expensive Range

Rovers, most of whom, we were told, worked for the government of the Falklands, which earns around £40–£50 million a year in fishing rights. No wonder there were so many flash cars. It was quite an aloof place and felt a bit like a closed society: you couldn't just go and live there if you felt like it. We also spent an interesting time at the Port Stanley museum, which was full of memorabilia and pictures from the Falklands War.

We spent the next couple of nights travelling to South Georgia and it was then that I thought I had better start to earn my keep. I introduced myself to the expedition leader and explained that I was the one booked to do the Tom Crean show. She looked a bit perplexed and then the penny dropped. 'Oh yes, I remember an email about you. So what do you want to do?' she asked. It dawned on me that I could have spent the whole of my cut-price journey keeping my head below the parapet and not performing at all. But where's the fun in that? Besides, these people hadn't heard about Tom Crean, as I discovered when I spoke to them that night. It had been agreed that I could perform the first half of the show before we got to South Georgia. So that afternoon I made a little announcement and asked how many passengers had heard of Tom Crean. I think one English guy put his hand up and there was a Canadian ornithologist who had seen my show in Swansea. I told everyone that I would be performing the first half of it for an hour after dinner. The ornithologist told everyone how fantastic the show was but I was pretty sure that they would all have come anyway: there was nothing else to do.

So, after dinner that night, my captive audience duly sat down at 8 p.m. My 'stage' was a little dais where we would normally hear lectures about the eating habits of krill or orca whales. I must confess that though these talks were often very interesting, I could never quite summon the same enthusiasm as my fellow travellers when a call rang out from the deck, 'Albatross!'. As everyone stampeded outside, cameras at the ready, Paul and I would look at one another. 'What? It's a fecking albatross. Who cares?' was our silent communication to one another. We somehow knew we shouldn't say this out loud …

I had brought with me on the ship a pared-down, touring version of the set, which was essentially the tarpaulin, the lamp, a piece of rope and my balaclava. And of course Tom's costume, which I always now carry in my hand luggage following the British Airways debacle. I did the first half of the show, which doesn't actually feature South Georgia at all. But nevertheless, the audience were on their feet: they loved it. When I chatted to them afterwards I told them there was a second half to Tom's story. At least ten of the passengers immediately went to the expedition leader and demanded that I perform it the following night. The Shackleton story went down a storm, too and so by the time the ship approached South Georgia the following morning, everyone was Tom Crean mad. This was very gratifying for me, especially since most of the audience had never heard of Tom beforehand.

The next morning they woke us at 6 a.m. to tell us we were approaching South Georgia and I made sure I was on deck to experience my first view of the island. I stood in the bow of the ship and watched those mountains rising out of the mist. It was truly, unforgettably, astonishing. Our first trip onto the island was to take a look at the fur seals, which were in the middle of calving. We put on our waterproofs, our layers against the cold and our anoraks, which were bright red so that we could be seen easily once we were let loose off the ship. We had already received instructions about island etiquette. So that we did not contaminate the purity of the environment, we disinfected our boots before stepping foot onto it. We had also received strict instructions not to answer the call of nature – any call of nature. Leaping behind rocks and hoping that nobody noticed simply was not acceptable.

We were ferried from the ship to the island in Zodiacs, inflatable dinghies with a motor. I would like to say that my first footstep on the island brought up all sorts of tumultuous emotions as I thought about Tom and his experiences there. But the truth is that the first thing to hit me was the stench. Oh the smell, sweet Jesus! Nothing could have prepared me for the overpowering aroma of ammonia (from seal and penguin poo) that seared my nostrils. None of those nature programmes ever talk about the pong, do they? I don't remember David Attenborough ever giving it a mention. It was a deeply, deeply unpleasant smell. I felt like saying, 'Tom Crean territory or no, can we go back to the ship please?' You get used to it after a while, although that smell lingered in my nostrils long after we left the island.

We were left for four hours to wander around looking at fur seals and penguin colonies. The fur seals were calving on the beach and you had to be careful if you walked among them. The young males in particular would run after you and I imagine that they could give you quite a nasty bite. The best way to scare them off is to make yourself big by holding your hands above your head and clapping loudly.

Then you run away as fast as you can. Physical coward that I am, I was quite relieved when I moved away from the beaches and the calving seals. You'd have to run pretty sharpish because those seals looked as if they meant business. Despite those initial challenges, it was wonderful to be there on South Georgia, looking at those remarkable colonies of wild animals against the stunning mountainous backdrop.

That night we sailed around to Fortuna Bay and from there we were going to retrace the last four miles of the extraordinary journey across South Georgia when Tom, Shackleton and Worsley finally arrived at Stromness whaling station. I was thrilled at the prospect and wanted to mark it in some way so, after putting on the layers of warm clothes, I put on Tom's Burberry.

Surprisingly, it did not feel as cold out there as I had expected. Ironically, it was colder back home than it was in the Antarctic. At the time, the UK was in the grip of an icy winter with temperatures dropping to below minus 5, whereas we were enjoying a positively tropical minus 1 or 2 centigrade on South Georgia.

We set off on our four-mile trek, looking for all the world like a colony of red ants in our vibrant anoraks. Well, apart from me, in Tom's Burberry.

The captain of the *Polar Star* was very taken with Tom and his story so he allowed me to bend the rules a little. We passed the lake that Shackleton had named after Tom because he had fallen into it, prompting the comment from Shackleton, 'If there's a hole to be found, Tom will find it.' It was a stunning sapphire-blue lake, sure enough. During our walk, people in the group kept coming up to me and asking me how it felt to be following in Tom's footsteps. In truth, I wasn't feeling anything at all because I was never left alone with my thoughts and emotions for long enough to gather them. I was constantly being engaged in conversation by my fellow passengers curious to know what was going on inside me. I don't wish to sound ungrateful: I was very moved that they were so fired up by Tom's story and was very appreciative of the fact that they were thinking about what this journey meant to me.

I paused for reflection when we came over the lip of the mountain and saw, spread below us, the whaling station of Stromness. It felt like a very special vista, barely changed in the last hundred years. A century ago that was the welcome sight greeting Crean, Shackleton and Worsley as they neared the end of their journey. I tried to imagine just how they might have felt, after all those months, to know that their torturous trek was nearly at an end, that they were so close to safety for themselves and, hopefully, the men who were depending on them. They had just heard the station's steam whistle and now they could see signs of other life, figures moving around below and smoke coming out of the station chimney. But they were not safe yet. To get down to the station, the exhausted men still had to negotiate one more dangerous obstacle: a freezing-cold waterfall. It took them hours as, tied together, they carefully climbed down the steep rock face. At any stage the ropes could have snapped or one of them could have lost his footing and the story could have had a very different ending. We, too, were going to go down the path of the waterfall, but instead of risking our necks trying to negotiate the fall itself, we would walk on the land next to it. Even this was no easy thing. For a start it was all slippery scree rather than grass. And as I looked down at how steep the descent was and how far up we were – it would be a bit like looking down from the top of the London Eye to the ground below – I had even more respect for those three men.

Walking sideways, we slowly but surely made our way down to the bottom. I stood and watched the waterfall for a while and contemplated Tom's last stagger to the whaling station itself. We were not allowed into the abandoned old station because it was too dangerous – the galvanised steel was so dilapidated it could shear off at any moment and literally slice a person in two. One member of our group disobeyed the strict instructions not to go into Stromness for our own safety. He was hauled in front of the captain and given a proper roasting. I did not really mind that I didn't get to stand at the door of the manager's cabin, the place where Shackleton had summoned the strength to spit out his name to the astounded Norwegian whaler. I was just happy to be there, in the same place where Tom must have been rejoicing all those years ago. I remember thinking, 'This is the same view Tom must have had after eighteen months of being adrift and not knowing if they were going to live or die. As he stood here, he knew, finally, that they could live.' It felt pretty momentous to be standing in his footsteps.

The ship was waiting for us at the water's edge and took us round the coast to Grytviken. Previously the site of a whaling station, this settlement is now notable because it is where Shackleton died of a heart attack on 5 January 1922 and where, at his wife's insistence, he was laid to rest. He is buried among whalers in a small graveyard surrounded by a picket fence, his grave marked by a block of rough-hewn granite. As part of a little ceremony

Aidan stands in front of Crean Lake and the foothills of the Allardyce range on South Georgia, December 2010.

to honour him, I read an extract from Shackleton's diary, written shortly after he arrived at Stromness. It says: 'We had entered a year and a half before with well-found ship, full equipment and high hopes. We had suffered, starved and triumphed, grovelled down yet grasped at glory, grown bigger in the bigness of the whole. We had seen God in his splendours, heard the text that Nature renders. We had reached the naked soul of man.' Beautiful words. Then came the toast: the ritual is that you have a swig of whisky and one for the Boss, which you throw on his grave. I threw mine on behalf of Tom, who never got to say goodbye to Shackleton.

As inhospitable as South Georgia is, there are a handful of people who live there. The British Antarctic Survey team stay there for two-year stints and, during the summer, a small staff runs the museum at Grytviken. That evening I performed my show for the survey and museum staff in the old Norwegian church at Grytviken. What the show lacked in theatricality – there were no stage lights – it more than made up for in locality and atmosphere. It felt amazing to be telling Tom's story just a fjord away from where he and his comrades finally found refuge after their eighteen-month ordeal.

We had a barbecue afterwards and, chatting to the British Antarctic Survey team, you realised that you had to have a certain disposition to be living in such a remote place. I heard that two years earlier, the whole crew had been affected by a failed romance between two staff members. On South Georgia there is nowhere to hide and many places the staff are not allowed to venture for their own safety. In the weeks we were there, we probably saw more of the island than most of them see in two years.

That night we were heading to Elephant Island to see where the twenty-two stranded men of the *Endurance* had waited for the Boss to return for them, not knowing if their six comrades had even survived the 800-mile journey to South Georgia. Our nights on the ship were now much more comfortable thanks to Paul, who had managed to get us upgraded to the Shackleton Suite, which meant a separate bedroom where Paul could snore to his heart's content and not disturb me. Paul had been to the Antarctic twice before and he said this time he felt like a celebrity because of his association with Tom and my show. Unlike a lot of the British passengers, who tended to sit with the same people every night at dinner, we would spread ourselves around and chat with different people like the gregarious Irish folk we are. Towards the end of the trip, however, even we tended to sit with familiar folk and they were generally the ones who, like us, were a bit tired of all the Tom talk and wanted to discuss other things. We met some fascinating people, including a woman who was into spirituality and reckoned I was channelling Tom as I performed him. She felt that Tom had appeared to her one day through me ... After dinner, Paul and I would be visited by spirits of the gin-and-tonic variety at the lovely little bar where we would enjoy a moderate tipple and sometimes a sing-song.

There was no singing on the night we travelled to Elephant Island because that was the night a force 10 gale had us rocking, rolling and pitching. The downside to being in the Shackleton Suite was that we were right at the front of the ship and high up and so experienced more movement than other locations on board. My handy little bracelet was no use to me that night. As a result of the gale, we were twelve hours behind schedule, which put the ship under time pressure to be back in Ushuaia on time for the next voyage. Sometimes planned excursions have to be curtailed or skipped altogether. But I was desperate to see Elephant Island and so was Paul, who also had another reason for wanting to go: he had promised his mother that when she died he would scatter her ashes all over the world. Some of her ashes were already scattered at the top of Mount Everest thanks to a sherpa Paul had met on his last Antarctic voyage. But as we approached the island in a Zodiac, his chances of getting his mum there were looking slim. With the water crashing all around the island, it looked as though it would be a very rocky landing indeed. The captain said he could probably land us but he wasn't sure if he could get us off again. Now, as I have mentioned, I do not do danger very well, so I would have been perfectly happy to have returned to the ship rather than risk life and limb. You really wouldn't have wanted to fall in that water: you would be dead from hypothermia in a minute and a half. And I certainly did not want to be stranded on the island, like the twenty-two men of the *Endurance*. That would be method acting gone mad. But the captain was determined to land me on the spit of land where the men had lived for four months and to see the statue of the Chilean captain who had sailed the *Yelcho*, the ship that rescued them.

With help from three other Zodiacs, he managed to land twenty of us on the island, at Cape Wild. It was incredible to think that here, not 300 feet from this eight-foot stretch of beach, those men had waited for all those four months in 1916. It was Shackleton's deputy, Frank Wild, who had kept up morale and kept the men going during those long weeks. He would begin each day by rousing them with the words: 'Lash up and stow, boys, the Boss may come today.' As each day passed, it was getting harder to believe it. Until one day, miraculously, up came the shout, 'Ship O!' What a sight it must have been for those men to be standing where we were now standing and to be looking at the smiling faces of Shackleton and Crean as they approached in the boat being rowed ashore by the Chilean sailors. 'Are you well?' shouted Shackleton. 'We are all well, Boss' came Wild's most happy reply. Wild is buried to the right of his boss in Grytviken with the inscription 'Shackleton's right-hand man.'

I was so glad that the captain of the *Polar Star* persevered in trying to land us on the island and felt incredibly fortunate to have been given such a fantastic experience. Paul, too, was pleased to have scattered his mother's ashes on the island. I took away a couple of small rocks and some unforgettable images. The captain said afterwards that we were one of the first groups to land there in about ten years because it was pretty hairy and most people did not have reason enough to take the risk. Maybe, after all, I'm not as risk averse as I thought I was …

The next stop on our Antarctic journey was Deception Island, so called by the whalers because it is not immediately apparent that there is any way to land on it. But we managed to get onto the island via the tiny sliver of a sound that was not immediately obvious. It is a fascinating place, a volcanic island, one of the South Shetland Islands, off the tip of the Antarctic Peninsula that borders the Weddell Sea. On the one side is a beach and on the other some deserted and decaying wooden huts that members of the British Antarctic Survey had to leave in a hurry during the 1950s when there was an earthquake. The tradition here is to take a dip in the sea and then sit in a hole you've dug in the beach. The volcanic sand warms the water that comes into the hole and within seconds it's the temperature of a warm bath. But first the hard bit. Paul and I were among the handful of people who took a dip in the sea. We ran screaming into the water and stayed in for a matter of seconds before running into our warm little dugouts in the sand. It was exhilarating.

Then we went deeper into the Antarctic, so much deeper in fact that it was light all night. I will never forget sitting out on deck at 1 a.m., bathed in a soft light and sipping a gin and tonic. We sailed down the west side of the peninsula and went on shore the next day to Port Lockroy, which houses the most southerly British post office in the world. Port Lockroy was a scientific base in the 1940s and 1950s and it was absorbing to wander around the old buildings, where people slept in dormitories with walls covered in pictures of Marilyn Monroe and Gina Lollobrigida.

We spent several days sailing around the Antarctic Peninsula and were treated to visual feasts of mountains and glaciers. Our soundtrack was the crack of glaciers calving, which meant we could never sail too close to them in case a chunk of ice broke off at the wrong moment. On one occasion, we got into the Zodiacs at 9 p.m. and went out in search of orca that had allegedly been spotted, but sadly we didn't see any. This disappointment was more than made up for the following day when we landed on the most southerly point of our voyage. It was here that I had a tiny notion of what it must have felt like when Tom took his life in his hands and, with his colleagues, slid down a glacier on his bottom. We were allowed to do the same thing – one at a time – sliding down a glacier that had a hump in the middle so you couldn't see what was beyond until you flew at breakneck speed over it. It was another 'Wow!' moment. After that we were landed on a piece of drift ice to see our last colony of penguins before heading home. The size of a school playground, it was a much thinner piece of ice than the one on which the crew of the *Endurance* had to live for months when the ship was crushed, but it gave us some idea of the precariousness of their situation. It seemed an appropriate time to do a little bit of Tom and so I performed the last ten minutes of the show out on the Antarctic ice.

Afterwards, the Zodiac pilot told me that he was going to take everyone else off the ice and leave me on my own for a while. Off they all went and, for the first time in the whole of the trip I was contemplating the landscape all alone. The Zodiac had gone so far away that I could no longer hear it and there it was, the Antarctic silence. Suddenly, I started to cry. It was the first time I had been overcome with emotion throughout the whole trip. I think it was the silence, the isolation, the sense of life's fragility that moved me so much. I also think it was a real moment of connection with Tom, not dissimilar to the South Pole Inn performance many years before, when I felt that he was really with me, showing me something real and true, showing me himself. Then, after half an hour the Zodiac returned and we went back to the *Polar Star* to begin our journey home. I was dreading returning to the waters of Drake's Passage, which had been so turbulent on our outward trip, but this time it was as smooth as a lake. Tom watching over us, perhaps.

I detoured to Buenos Aires on my homeward journey to do the mobile-phone plagued performance at the Irish embassy that I have already mentioned. Before the show the Ambassador thought I might like to meet some fellow Celts, so he took me to meet some Argentinian-Irish who were gathering at the annual reunion of the Catholic school they had attended. Now in their seventies, they were the sons and daughters of Irish immigrants who came to the country just before or after the First World War. They had wonderful names such as José McCarthy, but despite their Irish heritage, they didn't speak a word of English. By the time we got there, the *céilí* was in full flow and it seemed as though the alcohol had been flowing pretty freely, too, because everyone was very merry. None of them had a clue who Tom Crean was, but that was not important. The main thing was that we were Irish and in their eyes that was enough to make us celebrities. Everyone wanted to talk to us and, with the Ambassador translating, we passed a very interesting, if slightly confusing, two hours.

If I had no idea what the locals were saying to me, I also had no idea what they were feeding me. After the show we were taken to a local Peruvian restaurant and were given all sorts of morsels and little titbits, the like of which I have never seen before. Not all of it looked appetising or even edible but when in Rome ... That night, our plush hotel room at the Hilton must have looked like a Chinese laundry, with Tom's sweat-sodden long johns, socks and Burberry strewn around the room in order to dry them out before our flight the next day. As much as I looked forward to going home, I was sad that our marvellous adventure was over. But I now had a whole album of images to take on tour with me: the places that I had talked about and imagined for so long were now real, vivid pictures that I could conjure when I needed them.

It was a magical trip and I think it brought me closer to the spirit of Tom. There was one point when I even think I heard him communicating with me. It was when we were out on the Zodiac looking fruitlessly for the orca. We heard a sound that the expedition leader said she had never heard before and really couldn't account for. It was a strange, eerie sound, like a sort of windy whine. Maybe it was just the wind, but I prefer to think that it was Tom sending me a little message, approving of my visit. He was probably saying, 'See Aidan, this is why I went three times ...'

12
HOME IS THE SAILOR

We returned home to Annascaul where we opened a public house. But what to name it? Well I had the name, it was just a little dangerous as it alludes to my past, but I wanted to call it what I wanted to. You might know it, sure – it's at the bottom of the hill before the bridge off the road before the blacksmith's – and my name? THE SOUTH POLE INN – because I never got there, did I? But I thought, wouldn't it be magnificent to be upstairs, putting my collar and tie on, with my wife and two living daughters, and Katie in spirit, but for us all to be going below to work – at The South Pole.

From *Tom Crean – Antarctic Explorer* (Aidan Dooley)

I have always thought it an awful tragedy that, after all the times Tom eluded death, he had to watch his own daughter take her last breath. His middle daughter, Katie, was epileptic and on 8 December 1924, when she was just four years old, she suffered a fatal fit. Her dad could do nothing to save her and, as a father myself, I cannot even begin to imagine how devastating that must have been for him. One of the reasons that Tom settled so happily into his retirement was the joy he derived from being a dad. His daughters Eileen and Mary said to me, 'Our Daddy was wonderful,' and he was clearly devoted to his girls. He and his wife, Nell, are buried with Katie in a family grave that he built with his own hands after Katie's death.

When I first went to Annascaul to perform at the South Pole Inn during that memorable initial weekend in October 2001, Tom's grave was top of my list of places to see. The Ballynacourty burial site is situated about a mile and a half outside the village, up towards the hills where Tom loved to walk. It is a singular graveyard because it stands on a bog, which means that the dead cannot be buried underground because they won't stay buried. After a while the boggy ground will propel the bodies back up to the surface. So little cairns, like mini mausoleums, are built to enable the bodies to lie undisturbed on top of the ground. At the time of my first visit, the graveyard was quite wild and over-grown, with an assortment of unruly cairns made of rocks and stone. As I made my way over the brambles to Tom's grave, I was startled that I could see inside many of the rocky cairns, including the odd human bone or two. The Crean family grave is in the top right-hand corner. You couldn't miss it because, unlike most of the other graves, it was a solid block of concrete – Tom had obviously decided that he wanted to give his family some privacy.

The Crean family grave is a plain, square structure. At the front is a small metal door with a handle. It is through this door that some brave relative or friend would crawl in order to drag the coffin into the cairn. (It's a job that possibly needs a little Jameson fortification.) The side of the grave bears the fitting inscription, 'Home is the sailor, home from the sea.' Below a stone Celtic cross, three separate plaques bear witness to the people resting there. The top inscription is perhaps the most touching: 'In Loving Memory of our darling Katie.' I was struck by how warm and personal it was to use the endearment 'darling'. Underneath are the weathered words: 'In Affectionate Remembrance of Tom Crean (RIP) Who Died on 27th July 1938 / From His Sorrowing Wife and Children.' Sorrowing: such

The plaques on the Crean family grave in Annascaul, County Kerry.

CREAN

TOM CREAN
ANTARCTIC EXPLORER
DIED 27th JULY 1938.

HIS WIFE ELLEN
DIED 2nd JANUARY 1968.

THEIR DAUGHTER KATIE
DIED 8th DECEMBER 1924.
AND
THE EXTENDED CREAN FAMILY.

REST IN PEACE.
Home is the Sailor
Home from the Sea

OF OUR DARLI
KATIE
FROM HER FATHER
MOTHER AND SISTERS

AFFECTIONATE REMEMBRANCE O
TOM CREAN (R.I.P.)
WHO DIED ON 27TH JULY 1938
FROM HIS SORROWING WIFE AND CHILDR

ELLEN CREAN
DIED 2ND JAN. 1968
R.   I.   P.

a beautiful and evocative word. And finally, a simple plaque that says: Ellen Crean Died 2nd Jan. 1968 RIP.' Lying on the grave is a wreath of porcelain flowers sent by Teddy Evans, which was delivered in a Rolls-Royce on the day of Tom's funeral. An admiral at the time of Tom's death in July 1938, Evans clearly never forgot his debt of gratitude to the man who saved his life with such astounding courage.

As I stood looking at his grave for that very first time, I thought about the emotional investment in this block of concrete that Tom built for his little girl, about my own emotional investment in the man whose physical remains lay within it. It felt very poignant. I have visited his grave several times in the past fourteen years and each time is no less moving. Nowadays, however, the graveyard is much tidier. Since Tom Crean has been properly recognised and people have sought out his resting place, the council has built a proper path in the graveyard and encouraged people to tidy up their cairns, so many have now been replastered and repainted. Tom is buried right beside a little stream and it seems apt that he is within earshot of natural, running water. It's a fine resting place for him.

Another very significant landmark I visited during that weekend was the Black Lake, the place where Tom loved to walk his dogs in quiet contemplation. It is a trek to get up there: you have to go along little boreens, through a rickety gate until, at last, there you are. It feels like a very special place, very silent and remote, with the glacial lake as still as a mirror and mysteriously, darkly deep. Tom loved to walk round the lake and probably went up there most days. In fact, walking must have played a big part in Tom's retirement: as well as his walks round the lake, he made his trips to the railway station for his newspaper and met his godson John Knightley from school for a daily stroll. I don't think this came from restlessness, however. As much as retirement and domestic life must have been a huge change for a man used to death-defying adventure, Tom seemed to take it in his stride. Perhaps it was a relief to finally hang up his Burberry and not to have to put himself through such punishing experiences out on the ice. His adventures had left him with black feet, numb ears and problems with his eyesight due to snow blindness. He was, I think, happy enough to retire; he was ready. When Shackleton asked him to be part of his next expedition down south in early 1920, Tom declined. He was preparing for an altogether different type of leap into the unknown: family life.

Since returning from the Antarctic he had been promoted to the rank of Warrant Officer, which gave him a much better pension. And Tom had slowly been paving the way for his future. In September 1917, he married Ellen Herlihy, a strong Kerry woman who was the daughter of an Annascaul publican. In readiness for civilian life, Tom had bought a pub in the village of his birth. It was an old one-storey shebeen with a thatched roof and Tom's intention was to modernise it to provide both a home and a business for him and his family. He was retired from the navy on medical grounds in March 1920 following a bad fall that had a serious and lasting effect on his already weakened eyesight.

In one way, it was perfectly understandable that Tom should want to retire to the place he grew up, his home. He had even married a local girl. But on the other hand, it was not the most comfortable place, maybe even a dangerous one, for Tom to be at that time. I try to imagine the world of the Dingle Peninsula to which he returned. It was a hotbed of IRA activity, a place of guerrilla warfare, a place where convoys of Black and Tans were in danger of being attacked and where republicans on the run could find a safe refuge. Within a month of Tom returning, his brother Cornelius, a sergeant in the Royal Irish Constabulary, was ambushed in Cork and shot dead by the IRA. And into this world came Tom, a man who had served the English 'oppressor' in their navy. No wonder he hid his medals away and didn't talk about his exploits in the Antarctic. Those soldiers of the Irish republic who signed up for the British Army and Royal Navy in the First World War were considered traitors in Ireland. They had fought for the enemy and in this new post-war Ireland, with the War of Independence raging and then the Civil War, these men were treading on quicksand. Their knowledge of guns and weapons would have made them valuable members of the IRA, but they would never be trusted enough to be let in.

I think Tom would have had some protection from his large family presence in Kerry and from local woman Nell. But he knew what to do in order to survive: he would keep his head below the parapet and stay quiet about his past. Even then, his family was not safe. When Nell was pregnant with Katie, she was attending the funeral of a local republican when it was stormed by the Black and Tans. In the ensuing stampede, Nell had fallen over and was trampled on. It was thought that this incident caused Katie's epilepsy. Whether or not this was true, Tom obviously thought that Kerry was too fiery a place for an ex-British navy man with a young family. He and Nell moved to Dublin, to a bungalow in Drumcondra where Tom supplemented his pension by buying bits of property. He seemed to be pretty good with his pennies and invested in land and property so that his family was provided for after he had gone.

I heard yet another interesting anecdote about Tom from someone who came to see my show. The man had with him a book about Scott and inside it was Tom's signature, next to the part in the book where he is mentioned. It turned out that the man's mother had lived next door to Tom in Dublin – she remembered that he used to take their dogs out for long walks – and she had asked him to sign her book. His inscription was 'From your famous friend'. An autograph from a man who, just for once, did not have to deny his heroic past as he did in Kerry.

The Creans returned to Annascaul once the political unrest had settled down a bit and it is then that he rebuilt the pub, with accommodation upstairs. It seems extraordinary that Tom should draw attention to his past by calling the pub the South Pole Inn, but maybe this was his way of proudly showing the world what he had achieved. Even so, it must have been quite a risk to be trumpeting his polar past for everyone to see. There is a story I heard that may also explain why he felt confident enough to do so … During the 1920s at the height of the Irish War of Independence, the Black and Tans would often ransack houses, hunting for IRA men on the run and weapons. The story goes that, during one such raid on Tom's pub, they were amazed to uncover his hidden Antarctic medals and his Warrant Officer's sword. Yet another story says that Tom was up against a wall, about to be shot, when they discovered a British flag and let him go. Whatever the truth of the actual circumstances, it seems that the Black and Tans had uncovered Tom's naval past, which may have offered him a certain amount of protection as far as the troops were concerned. I have been told that at the time of Scott's death, such was his standing with the public that the outpouring of grief was not dissimilar to that shown at the untimely death of Princess Diana. So Tom, by association, was a man of some stature – to everyone, that is, apart from Irish freedom fighters.

However, if Tom's past didn't exactly improve his standing in the republican community, he was offered an opportunity to do so when he saved the life of a local lad accused of taking part in an IRA ambush. Two Black and Tans had been killed in the ambush and their colleagues came into the village intent on revenge. The Black and Tans dragged out two youngsters, shooting one dead because he let it be known that he was defiantly republican. Before the second lad could be shot, he said that he couldn't have done it because he was with Tom Crean, no doubt hoping that Tom's known background would give him some immunity. Tom was summoned and he confirmed that he had, indeed, been with the lad. Whether or not this was true, the troops took Tom's word for it and spared the young man's life. After I heard this story, I later asked his daughter Eileen if Tom was being truthful in giving the lad an alibi. She said: 'I don't know, but I did hear my father once say to someone about it, "I said what needed to be said."' The instinct for survival that had kept Tom alive in the Antarctic was still at work, keeping him safe in his own community.

Saving the young man's life may have given Tom enough credit with his neighbours that he felt safe enough to allude to his past in the naming of his pub. I also wonder if the name was partly a tribute to his polar mate Edgar 'Taff' Evans, who perished along with Scott on that ill-fated journey. Tom and Taff would often while away Antarctic winters dreaming of what they would do when they got out of the navy. Taff was intending to open his own pub on the picturesque Gower Peninsula in South Wales where he was born and it wouldn't be too wild a guess to suggest that Taff wanted to call it The South Pole. Perhaps, in using the name that Taff had always intended for his pub, Tom was realising the dream for both of them. Because Tom was such a modest, self-contained man who did not keep diaries and did not boast about his exploits, I have sometimes made educated assumptions about his reasons for doing things as I tell his story. In the end, he may simply have called his pub the South Pole Inn because he wanted to, plain and simple, and regardless of what anyone else thought. It is interesting, too, that he used the word 'Inn', which is so rarely used in Ireland.

When I was doing the show at the Olympia in 2011 I received a letter from a woman who gave me another insight into the world Tom came back to when he left the navy. The woman, who was from Dingle, arranged to meet me after the show for a chat and she told me that her father had been manager of the Royal Bank, which was a Protestant bank. When Tom returned to Annascaul, her father agreed to open a bank account for him. Many people in Dingle at that time would not have needed a bank account but Tom needed one for his navy pension. But why would Tom, a Catholic, want to put his money in a Protestant bank? Answer: because none of the Catholic banks wanted his business. It seems so unfair now that Tom's naval career and his extraordinary endeavours should be something for which he might be punished rather than celebrated, but this was the world he returned to in 1920s Ireland and, pragmatic as he was, he accepted it.

Politics aside, Tom was happy in his retirement. He left Nell and Eileen to run the pub and seemed to spend a lot of his time walking. This, in itself, would mark him as a bit of an outsider, an oddity. Tom's godson, the late John Knightley, who was such a wonderful source of personal information about Tom, explained to me how strange it would be for someone at that time to go for a walk, just for the sake of it. Tom lived among farmers who may have had to walk miles looking for a lost sheep or checking on their land, but they would not expend precious time and energy going for leisurely strolls. Sure why would you? I remember asking John what his father and the rest of the community thought of Tom and what he had done in the Antarctic. John told me that people simply weren't interested; they didn't care. These were folk who lived halfway up mountains in the sort of thatched cottages that people now think are so quaint but in reality are ferocious, cold, isolated, windswept places to inhabit. These farmers were too involved in trying to put food on the table and keep themselves warm to be listening to tall tales about polar adventures. They were living a precarious, by-the-seat-of your-pants existence. They were, if you like, battling with their own Antarctic.

One of the things that made farmers' lives a bit easier was that they started to sell their milk to a creamery on a daily basis. So for the first time they might have actually had a little bit of extra coin for luxuries such as a pint. It probably would be only the one pint, or two if they were lucky, during their one weekly visit down the pub. I will never forget my grandfather talking to me about this notion of the Irish being drunkards. He explained that, for one thing, a pint of Guinness was very expensive relative to people's wages, so you could not afford to down several pints in one sitting. I worked it out and the price of a pint was probably about a tenner in today's terms. My grandfather also described how, in the early 1900s when he was working and still living at home, he had to walk five miles into Galway and back every day and the only thing he would have to eat all day was a piece of bread soaked in fat from the frying pan that his stepmother would have given him. So on payday when he went to the pub for his pint, it would have an immediate effect on him and he would have felt drunk very quickly. That's not to say that some Irish folk weren't drunks, but for many people the price of drink would have been prohibitive and it was often lack of food rather than excess of alcohol that resulted in inebriated behaviour.

So back to the farmers of Annascaul, who made a rare trip to the pub. They wanted to talk about the price of milk and sheep, about developments in Dingle that affected them personally and might mean life or death. They did not want to hear stories about snow and tales of heroism in a place they never thought about and that was far removed from their own reality. John told me that the only people really interested in Tom's stories were the middle-class men: the doctor and the solicitor, who would come over from Dingle to talk to the polar explorer. Tom, who was not a big drinker, would nurse a bottle of Guinness and would sit in the corner with them and, in a hushed voice, would tell his stories. A hushed voice? After everything he'd done? Once again I am struck by what a different world he inhabited compared with our own. But he had a contented twenty years of retirement. As a restful contrast to his polar adventures, life was happily humdrum for Tom. Daily routine consisted of his walks, his riverside chats to the local children about his time at the bottom of the world, the occasional glass in the pub and, trains and tides permitting, a read of the English newspaper.

Frozen ears and black feet aside, he seemed to have emerged relatively unscathed physically from his punishing time on the ice. The only problem he had was with his eyes, which gave him quite a lot of trouble in his later years. Eileen and Mary remembered his twice-yearly visits to the eye hospital in Cork for treatment, which was paid for by the navy. In those days it would be no easy journey from Annascaul to Cork, around 90 miles. And his daughters remembered how, on his return, Tom would rap the table, exclaiming: 'Jaysus, that's an awful journey to put any man through!' He may very well have been aware of the irony – a sort of in-joke for polar explorers.

In July 1938, 61-year-old Tom was taken to Tralee hospital with appendicitis. But there was no surgeon there and he was moved to the Bon Secours hospital in Cork. You couldn't really say he was rushed to the Cork hospital because this was rural Ireland where the roads were not the best. Such was the nature of transport there that the train timetables for Tralee were a complete work of fiction, dependent upon and rendered completely unreliable by the tides, which submerged the track completely twice a day. By the time Tom got to Cork it was too late: he died of complications from his ruptured appendix. He probably wouldn't have died from appendicitis today. His death was barely mentioned in the national press, which gave him a standard obituary without any mention of his astonishing feats of courage and endurance. However, at home in Annascaul, his funeral procession was the longest ever seen in the district. Tom the Pole, as they called him locally, was laid to rest beside his daughter Katie. I have wondered who it was that had the honour to climb inside the cairn and bring Tom's coffin inside.

I realise that I have never visited Tom's grave on my own: there's always someone who wants to see the grave of the great man. But one day I will go there alone and have a little private chat with the man who has been my travel companion, my muse, my alter ego and my hero for the past decade and a half.

13
TOM'S LEGACY

And that Norwegian cried, they all did – these whalers who knew the South Atlantic better than anyone came up to us one after another and held our hands between their claws and ... tears ... They couldn't believe what we were telling them we'd done.

From *Tom Crean – Antarctic Explorer* (Aidan Dooley)

I remember being riveted to the TV, watching the moon landing as a boy in the 1960s. We had a small black-and-white TV and we had bought a gadget that you attached to the screen to magnify it. It also gave everything a greenish tinge. I remember waiting for hours for the astronauts to dock. You have to wonder how those poor TV commentators filled the empty hours as we waited, and waited. 'Have they docked yet, Daddy?' I would ask. 'Has it happened yet, Daddy? Will it be soon?' But it didn't matter how long it took: this was something worth waiting for. Even as a child I knew that this was something important (a huge step for mankind, even). I have thought about the moon landings in relation to Tom and polar exploration. In those days, what those men were doing and where they were going was just as extraordinary and groundbreaking as the moon landings half a century later. The difference, for those Edwardian explorers, was that no one could watch it and no one would be keeping in touch with you throughout your endeavour. The Antarctic expeditions would usually be serviced by a supply ship once a year, but the *Endurance* did not even have that safety net because the expedition had not raised enough funds. Once those men left Lyttelton Harbour in New Zealand in 1914, that was it for two years. They knew that if they did not complete their mission or if they got into trouble, the first anyone would know about it would be when they failed to show up two years later. The first Kathleen Scott knew of the death of her husband, Robert Falcon Scott, in March 1912 was nearly one year later as she was journeying, under false hope, to meet his returning ship the *Terra Nova*.

It is hard for us to imagine a world in which people would be lost, without any communication, not even radio contact, for years at a time. As a boy I was fascinated by the idea of those men who made the first orbit round the moon to its far, or dark side. During that time, all radio contact was lost. The world held its collective breath in that eerie silence when the radio waves went quiet. Who knew what would happen? What was on the other side of the moon? No one had ever seen it before or come back to tell the tale. It was, apparently, an extraordinary moment when Apollo 8 made contact after their historic orbit. I feel that those Antarctic explorers of the Edwardian Heroic Age were doing the equivalent of that fifty years earlier. Someone told me that it was only a year or two after the *Endurance* expedition that the first long-range radio was developed. How different a journey it might have been then. I think we cannot be impressed enough with what a gigantic step those polar giants took, what a leap into the dark and therefore how remarkable their courage and achievement. They were on their own and they could rely only on themselves to get them through it, which is just what they did.

If I have achieved anything with my show, I hope that I have helped raise awareness, along with biographer Michael Smith and others, of an Irish hero who remained unsung for so many years. He wasn't the only working-class man who went unrecognised for his efforts on the ice, but I think he was uniquely heroic. His courage was immense, his strength of mind and body superhuman, his common sense abundant, his good cheer limitless. I am delighted that Tom Crean is now on the school curriculum. A whole generation will grow up knowing who Tom was and just why he merits a place in Irish legend. I was very gratified to get a letter not so long ago from an English woman who had written a children's book about Captain Scott. She was publishing the book in Ireland too and was doing a tour of Irish schools to promote it. In the first school she visited, she said there was an amazing moment when she asked the children if they had heard of Captain Scott and the Antarctic. Up shot a hand and a little fella said, 'Isn't he the one who went with Tom Crean?' Such a story gladdens my heart.

During the time I have been performing the show, awareness of Tom has increased all over Ireland. The village of Annascaul and the Tom Crean Society have celebrated him, including erecting a bronze statue of him with his pups in a specially created garden. The Kerry County Museum now has a permanent exhibition about Tom, which showcases his medals and many other details about his adventures. The exhibition was opened by none other than Everest hero Sir Edmund Hillary, who was a big fan of Tom and made a rare visit over from New Zealand to honour him. It was only a few years earlier, in the mid 1990s, that the Tralee museum, which is located in the Ashe Memorial Hall – named after Republican hero Thomas Ashe – received a bomb threat for daring to fly a British flag during an exhibition about the Second World War. We have, I think, come a long way since then. I think the changes Ireland experienced in the last decade and a half have helped my show reach a more receptive audience. From when the peace process started in 1997 and more Irish started to stay at home, it seems that people were looking for a new kind of hero, one who wasn't political, and Tom fulfilled that. Had I tried to put on my show during the 1980s, when people were still being killed for being on the wrong side, I believe that many theatres wouldn't have entertained the idea of a play about someone who fought for the British navy. As it was, I was in the right show at the right time and people have quite correctly not seen it as any sort of political statement. I have been welcomed by theatres and audiences all over Ireland, for which I continue to feel very thankful.

On a personal level, discovering Tom and telling his story has had a profound effect on my life and all of it good. To me, he is an angel. I don't mean a vision in white, fluttering around with wings, I mean in the sense of being a force for good: a modern-day angel. I have such a respect for him, this man who was gentle with animals, could cry at the drop of a hat and yet was ferociously strong and determined, a man who could lift your spirits with his unfailing good cheer, who was still able to sing when the going got tough, a man who would lay down his life for his fellow men. In all of my research I have not read a single bad thing about Tom (apart from bad reviews about his singing!). His story not only inspired me to write a successful show, it has inspired me as a man. As I have looked through the world with Tom's eyes, I hope I have learned to see things in a more tolerant way. I have still some way to go before I am a 'glass half-full' person like Tom, but I hope I am improving. Tom was prepared to die for others and if only a tiny bit of his altruism has rubbed off on me, I will be a much better person. I certainly think he empowers, not just me, but the thousands who have heard his story and take strength from his courage and humanity. A man of few words, he let his actions do the talking, and what magnificent actions they were!

I personally believe in some sort of spiritual afterlife and I firmly believe that Tom is with me in spirit. I feel that he has some sort of spiritual connection with the here and now, even if it's just me having a chat with him before a show. I know it might sound completely barmy but I feel as if he has been watching over me, that maybe he is my guardian angel, or has applied for the job (you've got it, Tom). But even if you don't believe in spirits, Tom's heroism still speaks to people a century later.

Doing the show has been an amazing experience, personally, financially, artistically. It has given me and my family a financial security for the foreseeable future that I never thought possible when I was scrimping around for the rent as a jobbing actor. And with financial security comes peace of mind. I have spent long periods of time parted from my family while doing the show, but we are not the only family to go through long separation and it was always worth it. On that note, while I am indebted to Tom for what he has given me and mine, I must also thank my wife Miriam for her invaluable contribution to the success of the show. A gifted and beautiful actress herself, Mim put her career on hold for a decade to take care of our children Liam and Nancy while I was away on those long, long tours. She has provided the anchor, the secure centre from which I could journey. Now it's her turn.

As an actor, this show has totally fulfilled me. If I never acted again I would know that I have created something that has given me artistic freedom and a character that has allowed me to be the best I can be. I remember once, flying home from America, the turbulence was so bad that I was seriously contemplating my own mortality. It occurred to me, as I sweated with worry, that I had lived the life I was supposed to live and had no regrets. (Having said that, though, I was pretty keen to keep on enjoying it.) As an actor, you are only as good as your role; this part, based upon such an extraordinary man, was an incredible one. True, I wrote my own part, but it is Tom's story that has made it so special, so powerful. It has been humbling and marvellous to receive so many standing ovations, but it's always been about Tom. I feel proud of what I've achieved but in the end it all comes back to Tom. He was a great man.

Tom has enabled me to see the world, to experience some wonderful adventures and to meet some incredible people. After a decade and a half of doing the show and travelling the world, I am happy to slow down a bit. Apart from the fact that I don't have the same energy as when I first started, I don't feel quite the same urgency about getting Tom's name out to the world because it is now out there. There are still a few people in Ireland who don't know about him, but not many. The injustice that lit a fire in my belly all those years ago is no longer such a burning pain because the name Tom Crean now means something to a lot of people. It's a name that has its place in history and will never be forgotten. It was Michael Smith who brought Tom to life with his excellent and inspiring biography and hopefully I've maintained that little pulse of life whenever I do the show. If we have brought him to the world's attention, we have also brought him home, to Ireland, our very own hero. Not that I am ready to hang up my Burberry just yet. As long as there are people who still want to hear Tom's story, I will continue to tell it through my show. I love performing it and it feels like a privilege every time I do it.

For me, Tom will always remain something of an enigma. He was a working-class man who didn't keep a diary and who didn't much share his thoughts and opinions. I have thought about what I would like to ask him if I met him. Well, the insecure performer would love to say to him, 'Is what I'm doing okay, Tom? Are you happy with how I am portraying you and your story?' But apart from that, I would love to know what it was that drove him on during his solo trek to save Lashly and Evans. I'd love to ask him if there was ever a moment, at any time on the ice, when his optimism failed him and he lost hope. And I'd love to ask him if he really had a yearning to go to bottom of the earth, or if it was simply a way to earn a very good, albeit hard, living.

I once met a man from Baltimore (USA) who had sailed the Atlantic. He was as brown as a berry, skinny as a lathe and drank like a fish. He was a huge Tom Crean fan and just happened to be in Annascaul when I was in the South Pole Inn. He came to see the show in west Cork and we chatted afterwards. I asked him what it was like to sail a 38ft yacht across the Atlantic. He told me it took twenty-eight days and that the owner of boat was a keen sailor who had made his millions in insurance. I was intrigued to know what the two of them had talked about, all alone at sea for a month. He told me that he never met his boss. He would be on duty for four hours while the owner slept. At the end of four hours, their respective alarms would go off and they would swap places, and so it went on. The two men never discovered anything about one another because they existed in their own bubble. So I asked him why he had taken on such a lonely job. His answer was: 'Because I was paid to do it.' I think that, on some level, Tom would have been

Aidan keeps Tom company at the New Year's Eve party in Annascaul in 2008.

amazed at all this fuss about what he did. He was just doing his job, he might have said. And when, malnourished, exhausted and dehydrated, he volunteered to do an eighteen-mile trek, it was a pragmatic choice; he was simply the fittest man for the job at that time. That's maybe what he would have said, but we will never know for sure. All we know for sure is what he did. And that, by any standards, was simply phenomenal.

ACKNOWLEDGMENTS

- Jane Dewey who saw the potential of a performance on Tom Crean and was an inspiration to that process.
- The National Maritime Museum, Greenwich
- Michael Smith whose book *An Unsung Hero* published by The Collins Press has been a constant and essential source in the 'knowing' of and the 'being' of Tom Crean.
- Pat Moylan who risked much.
- Jon Barker of Barker Litho who has designed and printed for the show since its beginning.
- All of Tom Crean's family who have been a constant support.

ALSO FROM THE COLLINS PRESS

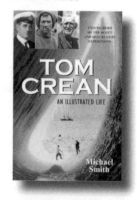

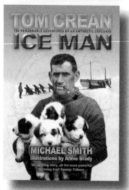

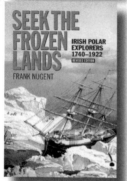

www.collinspress.ie

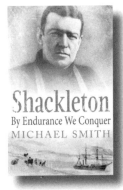

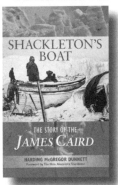

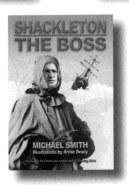